MYSTICAL PRAYER

The Poetic Example of Emily Dickinson

Charles M. Murphy

LITURGICAL PRESS

Collegeville, Minnesota

www.litpress.org

1	2	3	4	5	6	7	8	9

Library of Congress Cataloging-in-Publication Data

Names: Murphy, Charles M., author.
Title: Mystical prayer : the poetic example of Emily Dickinson / Charles M. Murphy.
Description: Collegeville : Liturgical Press, 2019. | Includes bibliographical references.
Identifiers: LCCN 2018059690 (print) | LCCN 2019022036 (ebook) | ISBN 9780814684948 (eBook) | ISBN 9780814684702 (pbk.)
Subjects: LCSH: Dickinson, Emily, 1830–1886—Religion. | Dickinson, Emily, 1830–1886—Symbolism. | Religion and literature—United States—History—19th century. | Prayer.
Classification: LCC PS1541.Z5 (ebook) | LCC PS1541.Z5 M85 2019 (print) | DDC 811/.4—dc23
LC record available at https://lccn.loc.gov/2018059690.

"Look no further if you are interested in gaining a deeper understanding of the holy mystery of Emily Dickinson's poetry. Weaving together history and biography as well as writings from mystics, popes, and poets, Charles M. Murphy skillfully explores the 'sacramental consciousness' of one of America's greatest poets."

— Elizabeth Johnson-Miller, author of *Rain When You Want Rain* and *Fierce This Falling*

"Charles Murphy's examination of Emily Dickinson's poetry in the Christian mystical tradition adds another layer to the growing corpus of serious treatments of her work as so much more than simply private lyric verse. In brief compass and with great care, Murphy enlarges our sense of the possibilities that Dickinson's genius lays before us. No one who reads this book will ever think quite the same again about her poetry."

— Paul Lakeland, Fairfield University, author of *The Wounded Angel: Fiction and the Religious Imagination*

"Charles Murphy's book weaves together an amazing range of sources: literary and theological, mystical and personal anecdote. It explicates Emily Dickinson's poetry with delight and sensitivity and raises the reader's awareness of her spiritual aspirations and fragile beauty of soul. It is an exploration of poetry and prayer that will be valued by all those who are drawn to either or both."

— Marie Noonan Sabin, author of *Evolving Humanity and Biblical Wisdom*

"Margery Kempe's autobiography was lost for 400 years. Thomas Traherne's meditations were rescued from a trash heap after the author's death. This book now demonstrates, more than 130 years after Emily Dickinson's death, how we're only beginning to see her poems for what they were."

— Jon M. Sweeney, editor of *A Course in Desert Spirituality* by Thomas Merton

Wild nights – Wild nights
Were I with thee
Wild nights – should be
Our luxury!

Futile – the winds –
to a Heart in port –
Done with the Compass –
Done with the Chart –

Rowing in Eden –
Ah, the Sea!
Might I but moor –
Tonight –
In thee!

Portions of this book were written in Rome, where I was the guest of the Pontifical North American College. I wish to express my thanks to the rector, faculty, and seminarians for their hospitality.

I dedicate this book to my two nieces, devoted physicians Karen Di Pasquale, DO, and Erin Dawson-Chalat, MD.

CONTENTS

INTRODUCTION:
Reintroducing Emily Dickinson

In 1830, in the small college town of Amherst, Massachusetts, remote in the Connecticut River valley, was born Emily Elizabeth Dickinson, who is regarded as one of the greatest—if not the greatest—American poet. Living virtually all her life in the Homestead, her father's elaborate house on Main Street, she wrote nearly two thousand poems, which she never intended for publication and which were discovered in a bureau drawer after her death. The Homestead, which was the town's first brick building, was where she, her mother and father, and her younger sister Lavinia lived until their deaths, assisted by Irish immigrant help. Having become more and more reclusive over the years, she died in 1886 at the age of fifty-six and was buried in the white dress that was her chosen attire in her later years. Her white casket was interred in the family plot at West Cemetery nearby. The headstone, surrounded by an iron fence, carries her name and, beneath the dates of her birth and death, the inscription "Called back."

Next to the Homestead is the Italianate mansion the Evergreens, built by her father to entice her brother, Austin, to join his law practice. Austin's wife, Susan, who was one of Emily's closest friends, composed her obituary, which emphasized that those knew her best understood her life, though lived in obscurity and without much exterior incident, as exceptional and rich.

The death of Miss Emily Dickinson, daughter of the late Edward Dickinson, at Amherst on Saturday, makes another sad inroad on the small circle so long occupying the old family mansion. . . . Very few in the village, except among the older inhabitants, knew Miss Emily personally, although the facts of her seclusion and her intellectual brilliancy were familiar Amherst traditions. . . . As she passed on in life, her sensitive nature shrank from much personal contact with the world, and more and more turned to her own large wealth of individual resources for companionship. . . . Not disappointed with the world, not an invalid until within the past two years, not from any lack of sympathy, not because she was insufficient for any mental work or social career—her endowments being so exceptional—but the "mesh of her soul" was too rare and the sacred quiet of her own home proved the fit atmosphere for her worth and work. . . .

To her life was rich, and all aglow with God and immortality. With no creed, no formulated faith, hardly knowing the names of dogmas, she walked this life

with the gentleness and reverence of old saints, with
the firm step of martyrs who sing while they suffer.[1]

After her discovery of the carefully sewn-together
fascicles of her sister's poems at her death, Lavinia said
she feared they would die "in the box in which they
were found."[2] She enlisted the help of a well-connected
friend in the community, Thomas Wentworth Higginson,
whom Emily addressed as "Preceptor" and to whom
she once addressed this question after sending him an
example of her work: "Mr. Higginson, are you too
deeply occupied to say if my verse is alive?"[3] Mable
Loomis Todd, Austin's longtime paramour, who had a
college background, was asked to go through the fas-
cicles and separate out the poems for first publication
by Higginson in 1890. Higginson called the suddenness
of the commercial success of *Poems* "almost without
parallel in American literature" and all the more amaz-
ing because the author "could not be persuaded to
print" and wrote solely by way of self-expression.[4]

In 1998 Harvard University, which houses most of
Dickinson's manuscripts, published the definitive edi-
tion of her poems edited by R. W. Franklin. This edition
collects 1,789 poems, retaining her distinctive capitaliza-
tion and punctuation, while previous compilations such
as that of Martha Dickinson Bianchi in 1930 did not.

In 2017, the Morgan Library and Museum mounted
a major exhibition on Emily Dickinson under the title

I'm Nobody! Who are you? The Life and Poetry of Emily Dickinson. The Morgan, according to a *New York Times* report, was instantly turned "into a pilgrimage site, a literary Lourdes, a place to come in contact with one aspect of American culture that can truly claim greatness."[5] On display, in addition to manuscripts of her poems, was the green-leather-bound Bible given to her by her father, to my observation heavily annotated and well worn. There were also a lock of her striking auburn hair and the only known daguerreotype of Dickinson. Sixteen years old, flower in hand, she looks straight at the camera with total self-assurance. At the exhibition's entrance was the oil portrait, done by an itinerant artist, of the three Dickinson siblings, Austin, Emily, and Lavinia.

The exhibition's accompanying catalog states, "The materials collected here make clear that the story of Dickinson's manuscripts, her life and her work is still unfolding."[6] The Morgan exhibition mirrors the strong assertions made by the poet Susan Howe in her book *My Emily Dickinson*; sweeping away prevailing characterizations of Dickinson as "a victim, a shut-in oppressed by patriarchal society and prevented from publishing during her lifetime," Howe describes her as a fierce and nonconformist mystic of Promethean ambition, a contemplative poet, reader, and scholar.[7]

In 1932, over a century after Emily Dickinson's death, her only niece, Martha Dickinson Bianchi, published *Emily Dickinson: Face to Face*. In it she describes their unique times together at the Homestead and her insights into her very special aunt, whose gingerbread she particularly enjoyed. She quotes her aunt as declaring that publishing her poems was "as foreign to my thought as firmament to fin."[8]

> To come upon her suddenly, looking up into the tops of trees, as if listening, not to the sounds of common day, not to her own thoughts, but to a mystic inclusion in some higher beauty known only to herself, forbade that we should fully interpret her. Nor was she lacking in a sort of spiritual arrogance—the right of one to whom much is revealed.[9]

The ever-elusive Emily Dickinson, it seems, always needs to be reintroduced. Terence Davies's 2017 film *A Quiet Passion*, starring Cynthia Nixon, captured well the inner life of Dickinson, whose exterior life was so notably without event. Critics praised the film as one of the year's best. One reviewer asked, "How do you dramatize a life lived almost entirely in the mind—and a death she foretold in poems so devastatingly intimate, it was as if a curtain lifted for her into another world?"[10] One of the film's most dramatic scenes takes place at the Mount Holyoke Female Seminary, where Dickinson was sent, at the age of sixteen, and remained for a year. The class stands at attention. Those who have joined the "saved" depart, followed by "those who need help." Emily is left standing with the few who are left, the "no-hopers." Back at home, we see the family gathering in the parlor, Emily sometimes playing a piece on the piano, the clock ticking, the darkness outside. At the dinner table, Emily's stern father asks why his plate has a chip on it; Emily takes it outside and smashes it. As an adult woman in another scene, she asks his permission to stay up at night to write at her desk. He acquiesces. She describes him as too busy with his legal briefs to notice. He does buy her many books but begs her not to read them because he fears they may joggle her mind.

A strong, vital personality emerges from the poems composed upon that desk.

> This is my letter to the World
> That never wrote to Me -
> The simple News that Nature told -
> With tender Majesty
>
> Her Message is committed
> To Hands I cannot see -
> For love of Her - Sweet - countrymen -
> Judge tenderly - of Me
>
> (*Collected Poems* [hereafter, C.P.] 519)

At her desk she discovers her truth, a truth of such "superb surprise," she has to tell it "slant" in the poetry so that it dazzles "gradually."

Tell all the truth but tell it slant -
Success in Circuit lies
Too bright for our infirm Delight
The Truth's superb surprise
As Lightning to the Children eased
With explanation kind
The Truth must dazzle gradually
Or every man be blind -

(C.P. 1263)

In 2018 a new recording[11] of musical settings—composed by Aaron Copland, Gordon Getty, Jake Heggie, and Michael Tilson Thomas—of some of Emily Dickinson's poems was given the appropriate title *A Certain Slant of Light*. Dickinson's personal "slant," her truth, is revealed in the poem beginning "There's a certain Slant of light," which depicts the oppressive darkness of the short yet endless days of winter in New England. One of her most cited works, it bears, as usual, no title. If one were given, it could be "Despair."

There's a certain Slant of light,
Winter Afternoons -
That oppresses, like the Heft
Of Cathedral Tunes –

Heavenly Hurt, it gives us -
We can find no scar,

But intentional difference -
Where the Meanings, are –

None may teach it - Any -
'Tis the Seal Despair -
An imperial affliction
Sent us of the Air –

When it comes, the Landscape listens -
Shadows - hold their breath -
When it goes, 'tis like the Distance
On the look of Death -

(C.P. 320)

To grasp such despair, we must understand her religious context, the still-vigorous Puritan heritage that demanded the public confession of sin to avert eternal damnation. This is something to which Dickinson would never acquiesce, despite strong family pressure to do so. A feeling of personal diminishment is the effect upon her existence of soaring cathedrals, which convey human insignificance over against the majesty of God. We're just "shadows" holding our breath until overcome by death. As a theologian I would describe such a spiritual situation as "believing unbelief"—the instinctive rejection, despite the cost, of religious conceptions that do not do justice to what we know to be the truth: that heaven is not supposed to hurt and humiliate. When St. Paul presented the Christian faith to the Ephesians, he prayed, "And now I commend you to God and to that gracious word of his that can build you up and give you the inheritance among all who are consecrated" (Acts 20:32). Build you up, not diminish you.

In this book I reintroduce Emily Dickinson's poems as examples of mystical prayer in the light of Christian tradition, and of St. Teresa of Ávila in particular. Those who discovered them at her death took them to be independent lyric poems, but I believe they were much more than that. She wrote them for herself—and for God.

ONE

PRAYING MYSTICALLY:
"I dwell in Possibility"

What Is Mystical Prayer?

Prayer is more than "saying prayers." "Saying prayers" (vocal prayer) from our church tradition and praying in public with others are necessary for us as social beings, but prayer is so much more than that. The experience of that "more" in what is called mental or mystical prayer is what makes oracular prayer, prayer with words, possible and meaningful. It is an awareness, beyond words to express, of God's presence everywhere and always, but especially to me. Jesus instructed his disciples to "pray always" (Luke 18:1). Mystical prayer, prayer from our hearts, comes from a loving union with God, or at least a desire for it. St. Augustine of Hippo (354–430) wrote, "Our hearts are made for you, O God, and they are restless until they find their rest in you."[1]

Jesus also told us how to pray: "When you pray, go to your inner room, close the door, and pray to your

Father in secret. And your Father who sees in secret will repay you" (Matt 6:6). In mystical prayer we go deeply within ourselves and discover God there. People sometimes speak of extraordinary mystical experiences, visions, and ecstasies, but these are not of the essence of such prayer. In fact the opposite is often true: God experienced as an absence, a darkness, even "nothing."

The church father Origen (185–254) was the first to call attention to the mystical meaning of God's words in Scripture. Beyond the literal sense of the historical text, God speaks to me now, revealing what St. Paul described as "the mystery hidden from ages and from generations past. . . . Christ in you, the hope for glory" (Col 1:26-27). All Scripture, both the Old and the New Testament, has mystical meaning, as Christ declared "even they [the scriptures] testify on my behalf" (John 5:39). According to St. Jerome, Origen surpassed himself as a profound teacher of mystical theology in the ten volumes of commentary he wrote on the Old Testament book the Song of Songs, a title that means the song most sublime of all songs. According to Origen, the Song of Songs, perhaps originating as a marriage manual, is the love song celebrating the mystical marriage between Christ and the church as well as between Christ and the individual soul. Concerning this surpassing love relationship, so evanescent and difficult to describe, Origen writes, "I myself felt that the bridegroom was approaching and that he was as near as possible to me; then he has suddenly gone away and I have not been able to find what I was seeking."[2] In an image that resonated throughout the history of Christian mysticism—as, for example, in the writings of another spiritual master, St. Bernard of Clairvaux (1090–1153)—Origen likened the experience of God to being bruised, to feeling yourself pierced with a spear of longing so that you long for him day and night.[3]

Evelyn Underhill (1875–1941), an early twentieth-century exponent of Christian mysticism, described it in general terms as the "ecstatic" (from a Greek word meaning "standing outside of yourself") experience of God. It is, Underhill continues, entering into eternal bliss, being healed and enlightened, a surrender to the purposes of divine energy and love. Going further, it is the experience of God in the whole created world based upon the incarnation of Christ, who in his person unites all of creation with God.[4]

In the Gospel, Jesus urges, "Look"! (Matt 6:26, 28)—just look at the birds of the air, the flowers in the field, and behold their divine creator. St. Augustine observed that God wrote two books—the book of creation and the book of Scripture, not just one, and that he would not have written the second if we had not been too blind to see his presence in the first.[5] It would be from this first book, the book of creation, that Emily Dickinson's mystical visions would arise, as well as from her personal sense of woundedness and longing. She once said "Consider the lilies" was her only commandment.

God's ultimate nature, however, is totally transcendent and beyond human words to express. When God appears to Moses, Moses is initially attracted to God by a fascination with the light from a burning bush. As a humble creature, he takes off his shoes in the divine presence. And when Moses asks God his name, God declares, "I am who I am" (Exod 3:14)—existence itself and the source of all that exists. Another interpretation is that no human word can express me, but you will know who I am by seeing what I do: my actions for your salvation, such as leading Israel to freedom from slavery.

St. Gregory of Nyssa (335–395), in his mystical text *The Life of Moses*, picks up on this theme. Gregory describes the journey into God as endless, a journey not, as one might think, from darkness into light, but the opposite—from the light into darkness. Drawn by the light he sees on the mountain where God dwells, Moses ascends, but once there he discovers the peak covered in darkness. His journey of faith will require that he step off the mountain in that darkness, with nothing to support his feet, to step into God.[6] St. John of the Cross (1542–1591), the contemporary and disciple of St. Teresa of Ávila, also describes this experience in his work *The Ascent of Mount Carmel*.

The Hebrew prophet Isaiah also speaks of faith's journey as an endless pilgrimage.

I will lead the blind on their journey; by paths unknown
I will guide them. I will turn darkness into light before
them and make crooked ways straight. (Isa 42:16)

Before the light, he describes darkness and the confusion
of unknown and crooked paths.

St. Thérèse of Lisieux (1873–1897) in her young life
knew such a darkness. She writes in her journal, "You
are dreaming about the light—about eternal possession
of the Creator . . . that one day you will walk out of this
fog that surrounds you. . . . [R]ejoice in death which
will give you not what you hope for but a night still
more profound, the night of nothingness."[7]

St. Teresa of Calcutta (1910–1997) chose her name in
religious life after Thérèse of Lisieux, the saint of the
"little way," not the great Teresa of Ávila. In 1928, know-
ing very little English, she left her native Albania to join
the Sisters of Loreto in Ireland. She was sent to Calcutta
the following year to teach in a school for girls, where
she remained until 1946. On September 10 of that year,
on a train taking her to Darjeeling for her annual retreat,
she had a mystical experience. Jesus instructed her to
found a new religious order that would go out into the
streets and serve the poorest of the poor. This diminu-
tive, humble nun eventually became the powerful inter-
national figure recognized as a Nobel laureate and
eventual saint. But like the little Thérèse, Mother Teresa
of Calcutta for most of her life experienced God in a

profound darkness of absence. In her journal published
only after her death, she revealed the depths of the pain
she experienced.

> In my soul I feel just that terrible pain of loss—of God
> not wanting me—of God not being God—of God not
> really existing (Jesus, please forgive my blasphemies—
> I have been told to write everything). That darkness
> that surrounds me on all sides—I can't lift my soul to
> God—no light or inspiration lifts my soul. What do
> I labor for? If there be no God—there can be no soul.
> If there is no soul then Jesus—You are not true. Heaven,
> what emptiness—not a single thought of Heaven
> enters my mind—for there is no hope.[8]

The theologian Karl Rahner, SJ, has made the observa-
tion that the "Christian of the future will either be a
mystic who has experienced something, or he or she
will cease to be anything at all."[9] It has also been said
that "a mystic is not a special kind of person but . . .
every person is a special kind of mystic."[10] In both these
ways, Emily Dickinson may be counted among the
mystics.

Emily Dickinson's Mystical Wrestling with God

St. Thérèse of Lisieux in her journal described prayer
as "a surge of the heart, a cry of recognition and of love."[11]
St. Teresa of Ávila defined mystical prayer (*oración
mental*) thus: "In my opinion it is nothing else than a

close sharing between friends. It means taking the time frequently to be alone with him who we know loves us."[12] But how do you pray if your heart is broken? And what if you believe that God does not love you and is completely cold and indifferent to your needs and concerns? This is the form of mystical prayer expressed in the poetry of Emily Dickinson. According to a biographer, her life situation required that she had to discover for herself "an effective mode of mapping the interior wasteland, to invent a verse that can address acute pain that has no transcendental cause."[13] On the other hand, Emily Dickinson always considered herself a Christian, and the God she wrestles with is not some abstraction of transcendence such as her contemporary Ralph Waldo Emerson proposed as an alternative to biblical faith. What gives her poetry such force is that she is wrestling with God like the biblical Jacob, who, unawares, discovers his wrestling partner to be God, the God who wounds Jacob to free himself and retreat into heaven.

> In the course of that night, however, Jacob arose, took his two wives, with the two maidservants and his eleven children, and crossed the ford of the Jabbok. After he had taken them across the stream and had brought over all his possessions, Jacob was left there alone. Then some man wrestled with him until the break of dawn. When the man saw that he could not prevail over him, he struck Jacob's hip at its socket,

so that the hip socket was wrenched as they wrestled. The man then said, "Let me go, for it is daybreak." But Jacob said, "I will not let you go until you bless me." "What is your name?" the man asked. He answered, "Jacob." Then the man said, "You shall no longer be spoken of as Jacob, but as Israel, because you have contended with divine and human beings and have prevailed." Jacob then asked him, "Do tell me your name, please." He answered, "Why should you want to know my name?" With that, he bade him farewell. Jacob named the place Peniel, "Because I have seen God face to face," he said, "yet my life has been spared." (Gen 32:23-31)

Dickinson, in her late twenties, expresses her spiritual dilemma in an almost indecipherable poem that speaks of two swimmers, most likely her divided self.

Two swimmers wrestled on the spar -
Until the morning sun -
When One - turned smiling to the land -
Oh God! the Other One!

The stray ships - passing -
Spied a face -
Upon the waters borne -
With eyes in death - still begging raised -
And hands - beseeching - thrown!

(C.P. 227)

One could read this poem as the actual chronicle of Dickinson's spiritual journey: she must turn back to nature outside of herself to save herself, because swimming out into God within is causing her to drown. The remembered trauma and pain of that experience inspire one of her most famous poems.

> After great pain, a formal feeling comes -
> The Nerves sit ceremonious, like Tombs -
> The stiff Heart questions 'was it He, that bore,'
> And 'Yesterday, or Centuries before'?
>
> The Feet, mechanical, go round -
> A Wooden way
> Of Ground, or Air, or Ought -
> Regardless grown -
> A Quartz contentment, like a stone -
>
> This is the Hour of Lead -
> Remembered, if outlived,
> As Freezing persons, recollect the Snow -
> First - Chill - then Stupor - then the letting go.

(C.P. 372)

The poem's beginning evokes a funeral service: the sitting around, the formality. But the ceremony is quickly invaded by severe existential questions about Christ's own death, the only parallel that comes to mind in her deranged state. She has tried to go about her usual life, but it is now all mechanical, her feelings having turned to stone. Life has become too heavy to bear anymore—like lead. She feels, if she feels anything anymore, like someone left outside to die in the ice and in the snow.

Where then can solace come after such a life-changing wound? How can she heal after her whole world has disintegrated?

It is in this context that we can enter into the ecstatic mystical experience of the later poem in which she, whom Christ acknowledges as his spouse, is joined to him by her sufferings and receives from him divine comfort and exaltation.

Title divine, is mine!
The Wife - without the Sign!
Acute Degree - conferred on me -
Empress of Calvary!
Royal - all but the Crown!
Betrothed - without the swoon
God sends us Women -
When you - hold - Garnet to
Garnet -
Gold - to Gold -
Born - Bridalled - Shrouded -
In a Day -
"My Husband!" - women say -
Stroking the Melody -
Is this - the way?

(C.P. 194)

The above version of this poem is in its original form as written in 1861. The revision of 1865 is what appears in Franklin's edition. I follow the insight of Dickinson scholar Helen Vendler that the second version, omitting the many dashes between words and the exclamation points, diminishes the poem's ecstatic rush.[14] In it, Dickinson acknowledges that her marriage to Christ lacks the conventional elements of engagement rings, the formality of being "bridalled" and of sexual union. But in her exalted rapture she has been raised up to royalty. She has been joined to the Emperor and declared by him to be his royal consort, his Empress—"the Empress of Calvary." She does not confer this title upon herself—it has been decided by God. Vendler, in her commentary, notes that this is an outrageous claim for Dickinson to make—divine conferral of the title "Empress of Calvary." Vendler concludes, "As she thinks up that designation in her small upstairs bedroom, she displays to us the unconfined sense of huge expanses of time and space natural to her imagination."[15]

Acknowledging her woundedness, Dickinson begins to see this spiritual condition as the releasing of her creative powers.[16] She is commonly known to have undergone a long period of depression, which would give a clinical description to this painful spiritual transformation of death to her old self and the discovery of the new, greatly exalted "I" inspired to write down her poetry. Poetry saved her.

A *wounded* Deer - leaps highest -
I've heard the Hunter tell -
'Tis but the extasy of death -
And then the Brake is still!

(C.P. 181)

Emily Dickinson lived her life entirely in the yellow brick mansion built by her father on Main Street in Amherst, Massachusetts, but she discovered within herself and expressed in her poetry an interior mansion much more opulent—with more windows and doors and made from fabulous material like cedar from Lebanon—such as Teresa of Ávila discovered. The "prose" of that earlier existence with its routine of life and social interaction was eclipsed by her discovery of Paradise, Being itself, her new domain. No longer drowning in, but embracing this vast horizon of existence, she ecstatically enters her own new, more expansive, and greatly more beautiful home within. She records the experience in this mystical poem.

I dwell in Possibility -
A fairer House than Prose -
More numerous of Windows -
Superior - for Doors -

Of Chambers as the Cedars -
Impregnable of eye -
And for an Everlasting Roof
The Gambrels of the Sky -

Of Visitors - the fairest -
For Occupation - This -
The spreading wide my narrow Hands
To gather Paradise -

(C.P. 466)

CONDITIONS FOR
MYSTICAL PRAYER

TWO

SOLITUDE:
"The Soul selects her own Society"

The Practice of Solitude in the Christian Tradition

The person revered as the founder of monasticism is St. Anthony of Egypt (ca. 250–356). As a young man, after his parents' deaths, he was attending Mass one Sunday with his sister. The Gospel passage being proclaimed that day happened to be the story of Jesus and the rich young man to whom he issues this invitation: "If you wish to be perfect, go, sell what you have and give to (the) poor, and you will have treasure in heaven. Then come, follow me" (Matt 19:21). Anthony, hearing these words, considered himself personally invited. After he made provision for his sister, Anthony's spiritual path eventually led him to a solitary life in the great desert across the Nile River where he would spend the rest of his life. But not at once.

On the fringes of villages in those days were small hermitages where committed Christians underwent spiritual training under the direction of one of these ascetics who had built the hermitages. Anthony joined one of them and spent his days in manual labor, his nights in prayer. He fasted, sustaining himself on bread, salt, and water. More importantly he engaged in what he called "weighing of thoughts," conjuring up and confronting memories from the past as well as his present temptations and unruly desires. Only then would he be able to endure the rigors of a solitary life in the vast and forbidding desert. At the age of thirty he felt he was ready for the desert.

Why the desert? People can become lost in its vast expanses, wandering aimlessly. But withdrawing into the desert allowed Anthony to see his whole life in perspective. The desert then became a place of healing, not only for himself but for the many others who sought him out there over the years. Anthony gained the reputation of being a healer of souls and bodies. Many sought his wise counsel and became disciples. When he died at over the age of one hundred, people were amazed at his appearance: his soul seemed to radiate out through his body. In 357, Bishop Athanasius of Alexandria, whom Anthony had befriended during a period of exile, published the biography that made him remembered.

In subsequent expressions of monastic life, groups like Teresa of Ávila's reformed Carmelite order created their own desert in the form of the monastic enclosure in which they dwelt. In its silence they could be attentive to the voice of God. The biblical prophet Elijah's encounter with God in his desert cave began when he heard a voice that said "Go outside and stand on the mountain before the Lord; the Lord will be passing by." Next,

> a strong and heavy wind was rending the mountain and crushing rocks before the Lord—but the Lord was not in the wind. After the wind there was an earthquake—but the Lord was not in the earthquake. After the earthquake there was a fire—but the Lord was not in the fire. After the fire there was a tiny whispering sound. When he heard this, Elijah hid his face in his cloak. (1 Kgs 19:11-13)

In this way the prophet tells us that God is discovered not in dramatic fashion outside of ourselves but by attending to the tiny whispering sound within.

In her masterpiece *Las moradas* (*Interior Castle*), written in 1579, near the end of her life, Madre Teresa of Ávila, the great sixteenth-century mystic and reformer of the Carmelite order, unrolls for her sisters her imaginative vision that within each of them there is to be discovered an immense mansion of many rooms and great luxury. It is no small pity, she writes, that through our own fault we do not understand ourselves or know who we are, created in God's own glorious image and likeness (Gen 1:26). Some even have souls so infirm and preoccupied with busying themselves outside that they are incapable of entering within themselves at all. So far as she can understand, the door of entry into this castle is prayer and meditation, she concludes.

Teresa admits that these interior matters "are so obscure to the mind that anyone with as little learning as I will be sure to have to say many superfluous and even irrelevant things in order to say a single one that is to the point. The reader must have patience with me, as I have with myself when writing about things of which I know nothing; for really I sometimes take up my paper, like a perfect fool, with no idea of what to say or of how to begin."[1] It is obvious, however, that she is taking great delight in this image of the mansions to be discovered within herself and others.

Her bottom line is that we must learn to understand ourselves and take pity on ourselves. Our soul's capacity is so vastly greater than we can realize. Since God has given us such dignity, we should allow ourselves to roam through this mansion within. The starting point, she emphasizes, is self-knowledge.[2] Let us walk, walk with humility, then, through these rooms rather than fly through them, she urges. But first we must be willing to put aside all unnecessary affairs and busyness, "the hurly-burly," she calls it, in order to be free. Then we are free to pray and to meditate.[3]

The American Cistercian monk Thomas Merton, in his *Thoughts in Solitude*, writes that to be our own person we have to stop allowing ourselves to be pushed around by exterior forces. We begin by entering into solitude, which, he says, is not just a recipe for hermits. Solitude allows us to live with our own contradictions rather than considering them a problem. In solitude we discover our personal calling.[4] In another reflection, *No Man Is an Island*, Merton observes that it is in solitude that we learn to be at peace with our loneliness and come to know the companionship of God. Through the practice of solitude we change our focus, returning to ourselves and to what is beyond ourselves—to God.[5]

Emily Dickinson: "Queen Recluse"

Near the beginning of Madre Teresa's description of the soul's inner journey to the discovery of God, she pauses to speak of those paralyzed souls who find themselves so overwhelmed with the events of their external situation that they cannot even reach the door of their interior castle, much less enter it. Eventually they may enter the first rooms on the lowest floor and outermost ring, but so many "reptiles" get in with them that they are unable to appreciate the beauty of the castle or to find any peace within it.[6]

Such was the spiritual condition Emily Dickinson found herself in before the breakthrough into poetry in which she discovered herself by writing. The depression, the general feeling of malaise, fell upon her around the age of twenty-five, just as the family was moving into their new home, the Homestead, and continued for the next two or three years as her domestic duties became overwhelming, due to her father's demands and her mother's incapacitation through illness. Her brother, Austin, was now married and had other responsibilities. But even more isolating for Emily was his adult conversion to Christianity and the social pressure of the religious revivalism that was sweeping through the country with such force that it was compared to the original Pentecost and the Reformation. Above all else, she felt the profound loneliness of having no one with whom she could share her deepest self or who could appreciate her uniqueness.

But then, around 1858, came a breakthrough, the beginning of a creative outburst during which she produced eight hundred poems in the next few years.

> I could not have defined the change -
> Conversion of the Mind
> Like Sanctifying in the Soul -
> Is witnessed - not explained -

(C.P. 627)

Emily was entering what Madre Teresa envisioned as the fourth mansion of the soul. Going now ever deeper within, she was becoming more connected with her true self. She was experiencing what Teresa describes as the "prayer of quiet" and effortless recollection. Her creative energies were flowing. She was in charge.

The Soul selects her own Society -
Then - shuts the Door -
To her divine Majority -
Present no more -

Unmoved - she notes the Chariots - pausing -
At her low Gate -
Unmoved - an Emperor be kneeling
Opon her Mat -

I've known her - from an ample nation -
Choose One -
Then - close the Valves of her attention -
Like Stone -

(C.P. 409)

Each stanza of this short poem has the unmistakable sound of a door shutting—thud, thud, thud. The poet has selected her own "Majority" of two, and no one else, not even an Emperor with all his chariots, can now enter. She has shut the valves; she has become unmovable like a stone.

In another rendering of this autonomous vision, the poet evokes nothing less than the biblical scene of the Last Judgment. But now it is not God before whom all humanity must stand naked to be shifted like grains of sand—she is the one who judges and who becomes the elect. This our "Drama" ("Tragedy" in an earlier version) here on earth may be brief, but she is the one with the power to evoke and carve the "Atom" of her choosing. According to one literary critic, "The stunning description of the timeless eternal moment in this poem was never surpassed by Dickinson."[7]

> Of all the Souls that stand create -
> I have Elected - One -
> When Sense from Spirit - files away -
> And Subterfuge - is done -
> When that which is - and that which was -
> Apart – intrinsic - stand -
> And this brief Drama in the flesh -
> Is shifted - like a Sand -
> When Figures show their royal Front -
> And Mists - are carved away,
> Behold the Atom - I preferred -
> To all the lists of Clay!

(C.P. 279)

Dickinson may be empowered to be her own self, but she does not feel the love of God within her, nor can she identify who God might be, he is so aloof. We sense her lingering resentment toward God who, after the drama/ tragedy of our earthly life, shifts us around like sand. Even the whole natural world in all its splendor and beauty is not at this point disclosive to her of God its

Creator. She, the poet, is the one who can tell us how to admire it.

> I'll tell you how the Sun rose -
> A Ribbon at a time -
> The Steeples swam in Amethyst -
> The news, like Squirrels, ran -
> The Hills untied their Bonnets -
> The Bobolinks - begun -
> Then I said softly to myself -
> "That must have been the Sun"!
> But how he set - I know not -
> There seemed a purple stile
> That little Yellow boys and girls
> Were climbing all the while -
> Till when they reached the other side -
> A Dominie in Gray -
> Put gently up the evening Bars -
> And led the flock away -

(C.P. 204)

The context for our understanding of the poet's spiritual dilemma goes back to the Puritan divine Jonathan Edwards, born in 1703. Edwards is remembered today mostly for his sermon "Sinners in the Hands of an Angry God." Its terrifying vision of eternal damnation generated in the 1730s what became known as the First Great Awakening. Edwards portrayed God's capricious will, his infinite and menacing freedom that allowed small space for human freedom in the face of divine predestination. Dickinson lived at the time of another Great Awakening. Her father, her brother, and her sister-in-law all felt compelled to make public confession of Christ to escape damnation. Dickinson, who had ceased attending church, refused to do so. Dickinson thus replaces the divine "I" with her own. She becomes the one who decides, both in time and in eternity. "I'll tell you how the Sun rose."

In a note to Dickinson's brother, Austin, Sam Bowles, a frequent family visitor whom Dickinson, by 1864, was declining to see, asked to be remembered to "the Queen Recluse" and extended his special sympathy "that she 'has overcome the world.'"[8] After her father's death in 1874, Dickinson ventured out less and less and reduced more and more all social contact. Her room was her cloister. One Sunday morning, which she customarily spent at home while others were in church, she led her niece up to her room, closed her hand on an imaginary key, and uttered, "It's just a turn—and freedom!"[9] Martha also recalls, "Once in that happy place I repeated to Aunt Emily what a neighbor had said—that time must pass very slowly to her, who never went anywhere—and she flashed back Browning's line: 'Time, why, time was all I wanted!'"[10]

The poet's embrace of what she calls "the silent life" is the subject of a poem in which her spiritual progress in solitude is achieved like the silent growth of plants.

Patience and effort are the requisites to achieve "Transaction," one's personal salvation, with faith intact. But in her version, no outside assistance is given or required in this desert-like existence. Helen Vendler says of the poem, "The examples in Christian history of a 'Silent Life' of growth were the anchorites living alone in the desert, and Dickinson here aligns herself with them (rather than with the evangelists, preachers, and hagiographers who diffuse popular versions of spirituality)."[11]

> Growth of Man - like Growth of Nature -
> Gravitates within -
> Atmosphere, and Sun endorse it -
> But it stir - alone -
>
> Each - it's difficult Ideal
> Must achieve - Itself -
> Through the solitary prowess
> Of a Silent Life -
>
> Effort - is the sole condition -
> Patience of Itself -
> Patience of opposing forces -
> And intact Belief -
>
> Looking on - is the Department
> Of it's Audience -
> But Transaction - is assisted
> By no Countenance -
>
> (C.P. 790)

THREE

ASCETICISM:
"The Banquet of Abstemiousness"

Christian Asceticism

In an essay written in 1960 and reprinted on the occasion of the Morgan Library and Museum's exhibition devoted to Emily Dickinson, the poet Richard Wilbur captured both dimensions of Dickinson's practice of asceticism under the title "Sumptuous Destitution." It was asceticism that allowed her access beyond appetite to the deepest desires of her heart, to what she described as "glee"—the happiness without cause that overtakes without anticipation.[1] She was discovering for herself what Anthony of Egypt learned about the perfection that comes from overcoming the unruly self through personal renunciation.

Dickinson and her sister-in-law, Susan, who lived just down the path, often exchanged books and discussed religious and literary topics. More importantly, it was Susan who was the recipient of many of her poems and whose comments were much treasured, even engendering alternative drafts. One book Susan lent Emily was *The Imitation of Christ*, the classic work of Christian spirituality second in popularity only to the Bible itself. This anonymous work, composed in the fifteenth century and commonly attributed to Thomas à Kempis, arose out of a lay movement called *devotio moderna*. Its pithy sayings, to be digested in small portions in the chaotic situations of the time of its writing, introduced a disciplined spiritual practice accessible to laity and clergy alike. "The life it describes," according to a modern commentator, "is one in which desire for Christ becomes more powerful than other passions, so that the ascetic discipline it advocates is experienced as a liberation rather than as a constriction of self."[2] The careful reading of the Scriptures that *The Imitation* recommends aims the reader at possessing the spirit of Christ through the three steps of understanding with the mind, relishing with the emotions, and conforming our life to his through our will. A new horizon for living is thus revealed: the highest wisdom is to despise the world and seek the kingdom of heaven. "Therefore," *The Imitation* continues, "withdraw your heart from the love of things visible and turn yourself to things invisible."[3] Antoine de Saint-Exupéry, the author of *The Little Prince*, echoed these counsels centuries later when he wrote, "And now here is my secret: it is only with the heart that one can see rightly; what is essential is invisible to the eye."[4]

The Imitation comprises four sections. Book One contains helpful counsels for the spiritual life that include combatting disordered affections and developing a love of silence and solitude. Among the directives for the interior life in Book Two are the need to look at one's self, the lack of consolations, and "the royal road of the Holy Cross." Book Three speaks of interior consolations, and Book Four of the Holy Eucharist.

It is enlightening to reread *The Imitation of Christ* through Emily Dickinson's eyes. You come across a passage that gives a stern warning—for example, "It is great wisdom to consider ourselves as nothing. . . . We are all frail; but think of yourself as one who is more frail than others."[5] Then, "Set aside an opportune time for deep personal reflection. . . . The great saints avoided human company as much as they could because they wanted to live for God in silence." Quoting the Roman philosopher Seneca, it continues, "As often as I have been out among humans, I have returned less human." The conclusion is this: "The only one who can safely appear in public is the one who wishes he were at home."[6]

The Morgan exhibition drew its title from one of Dickinson's most cited poems, which echoes many of these themes from *The Imitation*.

I'm Nobody! Who are you?
Are you - Nobody - too?
Then there's a pair of us!
Don't tell! they'd advertise - you know!

How dreary - to be - Somebody!
How public - like a Frog -
To tell one's name - the livelong June -
To an admiring Bog!

(C.P. 260)

In the copy of *The Imitation* belonging to Dickinson, the most annotated and underlined are chapters 11 and 12. "Jesus today has many lovers of his heavenly kingdom, but few of them carry his cross. . . . He has many companions to share his meals but few to share his abstinence," we read in chapter 11. Chapter 12 bears the title "The Royal Road of the Cross." In it we find admonitions that must have had resonance in Dickinson's life: "There is no other way to life and interior peace except the holy war of the cross and our daily dying to self." In other words, the only remedy is to endure it all with patient resignation. "The greater the height a person reaches in the spiritual life, the heavier one finds one's cross, but this is only because the pain of being in exile from God is in proportion to one's love of God."[7]

Emily Dickinson read such passages, and they obviously spoke to her spiritual dilemma. I concur, however, with this assessment of *The Imitation of Christ* by a modern commentator.

> There are some assumptions in the book, however, which do not fit most women's experience. Like so many male theologians before and since, Thomas à Kempis identifies sin with pride and self-assertion and love with unselfishness. Yet in recent years we have come to realize that this is a characteristically male spiritual awareness. The works of women mystics like Teresa of Avila and Julian of Norwich have helped us understand that lack of self and self-assertion may be the classic temptation for women. It is all too easy for them to lose themselves in tasks for others and never gain the inner spiritual discipline they need to center themselves. Had they been in communication, Teresa of Avila might have told Thomas that women must believe in themselves enough to develop their interior life, in order to avoid the very social distractions and negative gossip he found so deadly to the spirit.[8]

As we will note later, in chapter 5, Emily Dickinson draws on images from Catholic liturgy in her poetry. Perhaps Catholicism was a liberating idea to persons growing up within the confines of the New England Puritan tradition. We think of her older contemporary Nathaniel Hawthorne (1804–1864), a direct descendent of participants in the Salem witchcraft trials, whose novel *The Marble Faun* is set in Italy, and Rome in particular.

In St. Peter's Basilica a principal character, Hilda, finds a confessional with the sign "English" and there unburdens her soul and experiences forgiveness for the first time in her life. Catholic devotion to Mary, the Mother of God, becomes personally liberating and a protection from the power of an awesome God. As Hilda explains: "A Christian girl—even a daughter of the Puritans—may surely pay honor to the idea of divine Womanhood, without giving up the faith of her forefathers."[9]

Emily Dickinson's "Sumptuous Destitution"

Emily Dickinson faced many obstacles in her search for herself. As she once admitted:

Nature and God - I neither knew
Yet Both so well knew Me
They startled, like Executors
Of My identity -

(C.P. 803)

To discover the mansions within, she had to undergo the painful process of purging herself of the stifling and false identities manufactured for her. It required a courageous and perilous succession of *no*s.

No to the constrictive concept of women that her father imposed upon her, requiring her to either marry or simply stay at home doing domestic chores.

No to a cold household considering it to be normal that each person, as her sister Lavinia once admitted, stay in her separate room like an "Empress."

No to a dominating Calvinist ideology of religion making God into an arbitrary dictator of human fate.

No to a mandarin life of wealth and privilege in which the hired help were considered serfs.

No to a continued existence of fragmentation and woundedness, of desires never satisfied.

No to allowing her poetry to be published.

No to herself: "I'm Nobody!"

We can appreciate now in retrospect as an annihilation of this false self her repudiation of marriage, her refusal to have her poetry published, her instruction that all her personal correspondence be destroyed at her death. She strove through writing poetry to uncover her true yet elusive and mysterious self, but her indifference to its publication puzzled friends like Samuel Bowles, with whom she shared some of it. She referred to it as her "Snow," which for her meant "No"—the *no* of her renunciation of God and mammon.[10]

Publication - is the Auction
Of the Mind of Man -
Poverty - be justifying
For so foul a thing

Possibly - but We - would rather
From Our Garret go

White - unto the White Creator -
Than invest - Our Snow -

(C.P. 788)

Through her self-denial Dickinson was purifying what success could mean for her. As she wrote,

Success is counted sweetest
By those who ne'er succeed.
To comprehend a nectar
Requires sorest need.

(C.P. 112)

Dickinson's life of suffering and renunciation prompted a poem evoking the inspiring example of the early Christian martyrs. Like them she had experienced un-expected and potentially destructive "convulsions" out of the blue—in her case potential loss of eyesight, anxiety, self-doubt, withdrawal from society, loss of friends—but none had harmed them because of their unwavering faith. As martyrs they had risked every-thing but trusted in their betrothal to God. But for Dickinson at this point in her life God remains a cold and remote presence, less a presence than an absence.

Through the Straight Pass of Suffering
The Martyrs even trod -

Their feet opon Temptation -
Their faces - opon God -

A Stately - Shriven Company -
Convulsion playing round -
Harmless as Streaks of Meteor -
Opon a Planet's Bond -

Their faith the Everlasting Troth -
Their Expectation - fair -
The Needle to the North Degree
Wades so - through Polar Air -

(C.P. 187)

It is obvious, when we recall her adorning herself exclusively in white in the last phase of her life—another manifestation of self-dramatization—that Dickinson's personal asceticism was only partially successful. In order to accomplish this she had to confront her own egotism, her tendency to self-dramatization, her personal neediness (no one, it is said, ever sufficiently reciprocated her love and her desire for friendship).

FOUR

PLACE:
"I see - New Englandly"

The Christian Doctrine of Creation

Along with the spiritual practices of solitude and asceticism, a personal connection with a particular place in the universe is a necessary prelude to mystical prayer. Without this connection we would be lost in space, inner and outer. It is significant that we speak of St. Anthony of Egypt, St. Francis of Assisi, St. Teresa of Ávila, St. Thérèse of Lisieux, and Emily Dickinson of Amherst. The publication accompanying a recent exhibition on the poet's life has the apt title *The Networked Recluse: The Connected World of Emily Dickinson*.[1] The environmentalist, poet, and writer Wendell Berry observed wisely that we cannot know who we are until we know where we are. The poet Wallace Stevens wrote, "The greatest poverty is not to live / In a physical world."[2] A Dickinson biographer made this accurate assessment: "Standing in Amherst, Emily Dickinson could look into the heart of Eternity."[3]

In his *Spiritual Exercises*, St. Ignatius of Loyola (1491–1556), who was canonized at the same time as Teresa of Ávila in 1622, incorporates into his meditation techniques what he calls "composition of place." The person meditating upon a biblical passage must imaginatively enter, as a contemporary being personally addressed, the scene described in the passage. Locating oneself in a particular place over a significant period of time is critical to all spiritual development.

In the culture of nineteenth-century Protestantism, the doctrine of the world as God's creation was in eclipse. After the battles of the Reformation, emphasis in Christian life and worship fell upon Christ's suffering and death and our need for redemption. In recent times there has been a recovery, helped by evolutionary science and the pressure of the environmental crisis, of the fundamental significance of the universe as God's creation. It is of significance, for example, that Emily Dickinson was a contemporary of Charles Darwin and studied geology, which helped to open her thought to the glories and mystery of the natural world around her. In his encyclical letter *Laudato Si'*, the title of which was taken from the "Canticle of the Creatures" written by St. Francis of Assisi, Pope Francis writes, "It is our humble conviction that the divine and the human meet in the slightest detail in the seamless garment of God's creation, in the least speck of dust of our planet."[4]

The Cistercian monk Gilbert of Hoyland (d. 1172) insightfully wrote, "We have to pass beyond human experience but only a little to experience union with God. The divine majesty immeasurably transcends every creature, yet it is as if the divine majesty is close and familiar."[5] This "only a little" is Emily Dickinson's impetus and the abiding conviction embodied in all her poetry.

The book of Genesis contains not one but two accounts of creation. They are placed side by side, and no attempt is made to make them harmonize. In the first, which is actually the more recent, creation is depicted in theological terms. The creation is said to take place over six "days"; God sets the stage during the first set of three and in the second three assembles the various creatures to inhabit it, culminating in the creation of man on the sixth day. "God looked at everything he had made, and he found it very good" (Gen 1:31). Humans are unique, the only ones made in God's "image" and "likeness" (Gen 1:26). The seventh day is reserved for a weekly celebration of God's creation by observance of Sabbath rest. Many religions have their festivals—only Judaism has a holiday every week of the year.

In the second, more primitive account of creation, Genesis 2 and 3, it is the human creature whom God calls first into existence, physically forming him out of the clay of the earth and blowing into his nostrils the breath of life (Gen 2:7). God then creates a beautiful garden oasis in the desert, commissions the man to cultivate and care for it, and gives him first animals to name and then a woman as his equal partner (Gen 2:15, 18ff.). God with great risk endows humans alone with freedom, the ability to say no, even to God. And they do say no. As this second story of the creation continues, God, having taken a siesta, is taking a refreshing walk in the garden one late afternoon and discovers that the man and the woman have hidden themselves out of shame for their disobedience (Gen 3:8ff.). The humans' misuse of freedom has destroyed the easy communication and familiarity between them and God.

In his commentary on Genesis in his inaugural homily as pope, Pope Benedict XVI declares, "Each of us is willed, each of us is loved, each of us is necessary."[6] Nature in Christian belief is creation, a conscious mirror and reflection of the intentions of God, who willed all things into being out of love. Pope Francis then can draw this conclusion:

> The history of our friendship with God is always linked to particular places which take on an intensely personal meaning; we all remember places, and revisiting those places does us much good. Anyone who has grown up in the hills or used to sit by a spring to drink, or played outdoors in the neighborhood square, going

back to these places is a chance to recover something of their true selves. According to the philosopher Paul Ricoeur, "I express myself in expressing the world; in my effort to decipher the sacredness of the world, I explore my own."[7]

Near the end of *Laudato Si'*, Pope Francis draws upon the mystical insights of St. John of the Cross, the disciple of St. Teresa of Ávila.

St. John of the Cross taught that all of the goodness present in the realities and experiences of this world "is present in God eminently and infinitely, or more properly, in each of these sublime realities is God." This is not because the finite things of this world are really divine, but because the mystic experiences the intimate connection between God and all beings, and thus feels that "all things are God." Standing awe-struck before a mountain, he or she cannot separate this experience from God, and perceives that the interior awe being lived has to be entrusted to the Lord: "Mountains have heights and they are plentiful, vast, beautiful, graceful, bright and fragrant. These mountains are what my Beloved is to me. Lonely valleys are quiet, pleasant, cool, shady and flowing with fresh water; in the variety of their groves and in the sweet song of the birds, they afford abundant recreation and delight to the senses, and in their solitude and silence they refresh us and give rest. These valleys are what my Beloved is to me."[8]

Emily Dickinson:
"Beauty crowds me till I die" (C.P. 1687)

Among America's greatest poets Emily Dickinson's poetry stands out as the most popular and accessible. This is largely due to her meditations upon the natural world. When I was teaching a group of fourth and fifth graders years ago, I invited each to select a poem of Dickinson's and then turn it into a watercolor drawing. The results were superb. I recall one child's drawing in particular based upon a poem that begins

> We like March - his Shoes are Purple -
> He is new and high -
> Makes he Mud for Dog and Peddler -
> Makes he Forest dry -

(C.P. 1194)

Those of us who live in New England know that here the poet is dissembling. We don't particularly like March even though his shoes are purple. March may be spring on the calendar, but here it is what we still refer to as "mud time," which her poem references, the seemingly interminable interlude between a winter that seems never to end and the arrival at last of summer.

Spring's much-anticipated arrival is the subject of another reflection that expresses both the poet's anticipation and her ultimate disappointment.

New feet within my garden go -
New fingers stir the sod -
The Troubadour opon the Elm
Betrays the solitude.

New Children play opon the green -
New Weary sleep below -
And still the pensive Spring returns -
And still the punctual snow!

(C.P. 79)

The poem proffers a deceptive optimism, rolling out the succession of "New," "New," "New." There are stirrings now in the garden, and the birds are making their return from the South. Children are at last released from their winter confinement to play outside, and the spring thaw allows those who died during the long winter and whose bodies have been stored above the frozen ground to be buried.

But all of this newness is only a cover-up, the betrayal of our hopes, the unending "solitude" of our existence. Spring's return does not bring hope but only makes us more "pensive." The "punctual snow" is never far away. More snow is always on the horizon. In this poem nature is not the benevolent consolation as portrayed in Romantic poetry and in Emerson's philosophy. It is cold and threatening, its ominous reality portending not new life but the inevitability of personal annihilation.

Susan Dickinson, upon learning of her sister-in-law's death next door, immediately wrote down the first impressions Emily Dickinson made upon her:

1. Affection her strength.

2. Love of flowers.

Emily Dickinson was known among the people of Amherst as a gardener. They might glimpse her even at night attending her gardens with a lamp because the daylight sun was too harsh on her weakened eyes. Among the favorite New England flowers she planted in the exterior gardens were peonies, asters, baby's breath, bleeding heart, forget-me-not, heliotrope, hollyhocks, nasturtium, primrose, salvia, and snapdragon—and, of course, there had to be violets, marigolds, sweet peas, lilacs, and daisies. Just as St. Francis of Assisi did, she reserved a large section for wildflowers. More fragrant and exotic plants filled the shelves of the conservatory built by her father next to the house: gardenias, camellias, fuchsia, oleander, pomegranates, amaryllis, and jasmine. The passionate jasmine she reserved as a gift for her male friend Samuel Bowles. At the age of fourteen Dickinson had assembled an herbarium containing four hundred species of local plants. All the windowsills of her one bed-sitting room had plants upon them.

The years during which Dickinson's planting and caring for plants took place coincided with the high point of extraordinary gardens in New England, among them Mount Auburn Cemetery in Cambridge, Massachusetts, inspired by the Transcendentalists. In her teenage years, long before she discovered poetry, Emily Dickinson became fascinated with botany at Mount Holyoke Academy through its founder and first principal, Mary Lyon. With Lyon's guidance Dickinson collected, studied, and preserved 424 specimens of mostly local flowers, which she preserved in a large, leatherbound volume annotated with her own handwritten descriptions. On its very first page she placed an exotic jasmine—a tropical plant foreign to New England. No doubt the jasmine represented some of the volcanic forces within, her passionate capacity for love and risk.

The Homestead in which she lived she called "a house full of weather." From the four large windows of her room facing south and west, she could observe the surrounding landscape and its weather, the weather of nature mirroring the changing weather of her soul. This particular view of nature that presented itself to her every day upon her rising inspired a poem, or rather poems within a poem, reflecting upon the changing seasons of the year.

> The Angle of the Landscape -
> That every time I wake -
> Between my Curtain and the Wall
> Opon an ample Crack -

Like a Venetian - waiting -
Accosts my open eye -
Is just a Bough of Apples -
Held slanting, in the Sky -

The Pattern of a Chimney -
The Forehead of a Hill -
Sometimes - a Vane's Forefinger -
But that's - Occasional -

The Seasons - shift - my Picture -
Opon my Emerald Bough,
I wake - to find no - Emeralds -
Then - Diamonds - which the Snow

From Polar Caskets - fetched me -
The Chimney - and the Hill -
And just the Steeple's finger -
These - never stir at all -

(C.P. 578)

Every morning the poet finds herself "accosted," con-
fronted by a panoply not of her own making. Her view
of this expanse is constricted, in fact just a "crack." She
sees an apple tree whose apples are so luxuriant they
remind her of the Venetian fabric a bride might wear.
She gazes on inanimate objects close by and observes
the chimney's molding, the top of a hill in the distance,
a weather vane (Protestant church steeples were capped

not with a cross but with a weather vane). From this same vantage point she notes how the landscape changes from summer to fall to winter. The apples are gone, in their place only hard diamonds made of snow. The immovable chimney still stands along with the church steeple in this polar atmosphere, but nothing stirs. The church itself, like all of nature, is frozen in death.

Bereft of the church's consolations—the steeple is just a "finger" pointing nowhere—the poet looks for God in the natural world and finds only premonitions of her own mortality and ultimate extinction. At this point Dickinson is still far from entering the deepest chambers of her interior mansion as described in St. Teresa's fable, where she may deservedly feel cherished and loved at last and recognize her own beauty.

But nature, considered in Christian belief to be not just nature but the creation of God, also entered Dickinson's consciousness as she looked out her window. During the autumn of 1851 Amherst experienced spectacular displays of the aurora borealis. She was filled with awe. This nighttime experience occasioned one of her most famous poems.

Of Bronze - and Blaze -
The North - tonight -
So adequate - it forms -
So preconcerted with itself -

So distant - to alarms -
An Unconcern so sovreign
To Universe, or me -
Infects my simple spirit
With Taints of Majesty -
Till I take vaster attitudes -
And strut opon my stem -
Disdaining Men, and Oxygen,
For Arrogance of them -

My Splendors, are Menagerie -
But their Competeless Show
Will entertain the Centuries
When I, am long ago,
An Island in dishonored Grass -
Whom none but Daisies, know -

(C.P. 319)

In the first part of the poem this fabulous display in the
sky deflects upon her its own majesty. Though a humble
little flower on its stem in the field, she finds herself
"strutting" with pride and transferred self-importance.
But in the poem's second section she is overcome with
humility, recognizing that her own creative works are
by comparison a mere "menagerie" of disconnected
things. The magnificence of creation will continue to
dazzle eternally when she is long gone and buried, for-
gotten beneath the grass.

An earlier version of this poem speaks of beetles, not daisies in the grass. "Daisy" in fact was one of the nicknames Dickinson gave herself, but the humble beetle seems more apposite to one suffering the "dishonor" of human mortality.

Edward Dickinson, her father, died in June 1874. Life at the Homestead had gone on until then with quiet regularity. Emily Norcross Dickinson, her mother, passed away in 1882 after a stroke followed by a long illness, during which her daughter Emily was the principal caregiver. Vinnie, her other daughter, performed most of the social contacts, while Emily more and more retreated into solitude. Her poetry became less frequent, less intense. She seemed more taken up with domestic chores. From the mid-1860s and early 1870s, according to her biographer Cynthia Griffin Wolff, a new poetry of faith had emerged.[9]

It was at this time that Dickinson composed a poem that manifested a view of death more generous and tolerant of Christian belief.

Ample make this Bed -
Make this Bed with Awe -
In it wait till Judgment break
Excellent and Fair.

Be it's Mattrass straight -
Be it's Pillow round -

> Let no Sunrise' yellow noise
> Interrupt this Ground -

(C.P. 804)

More and more Dickinson came to appreciate the divine generosity revealed in the Christian doctrine of the incarnation: God actually becoming human and dwelling with us in the person of Christ. "The Divinity," Wolff observes, "is available in the familiar surroundings of one's own home."[10] In a poem of her final years Dickinson seems to repudiate the premise of her earlier "The Soul selects her own Society."

> The Soul should always stand ajar
> That if the Heaven inquire
> He will not be obliged to wait
> Or shy of troubling Her
>
> Depart, before the Host have slid
> The Bolt unto the Door
> To search for the accomplished Guest,
> Her Visitor, no more -

(C.P. 1017)

God is not shut up in his high heaven. God is at our very door. This poem shows the poet's development over time: awe for God's beautiful and powerful work of creation rather than anger and isolation; hope in eternal life instead of despair over human extinction; and an awareness of divine closeness that is so intimate that it gives a whole new meaning to being human.

In a very early poem, Dickinson wrote a riff on the traditional Christian prayer the Sign of the Cross. That prayer reads "In the Name of the Father and of the Son and of the Holy Spirit." It does not read "Names" but "Name," for God is One. Her version goes:

> In the name of the Bee -
> And of the Butterfly -
> And of the Breeze - Amen!

(C.P. 23)

The critic Helen Vendler judges the poem to be consciously blasphemous, a deliberate parody of the original prayer. The Father becomes a buzzing bee, the Son a flimsy butterfly, the Holy Spirit a passing breeze: the Blessed Trinity reduced to three *B*s.

But the resonances between the divine figures and their representations in nature are very real and revealing. The bee is a source of energy and initiative as is God the Father, the Creator of the heavens and the earth. The butterfly in Christian iconography is the symbol of the everlasting life won for us by the life, death, and resurrection of Christ. And the breeze—what else but the powerful wind of Pentecost when the Holy Spirit first descended? What a clever way—and so typical of

Dickinson, lover of the natural world—to underscore the declaration in the psalms: "The heavens declare the glory of God and the firmament proclaims his handiwork" (Ps 19:1).

In these ways over many years we watch with awe Emily Dickinson's spiritual awareness developing in the village of Amherst to such an extent that she achieves entrance into the innermost mansion of her soul, described by St. Teresa, where she discovers her unique beauty as God's own beloved bride. God, it turns out, is as familiar as the figure in the second creation account in the book of Genesis taking his afternoon stroll in the garden after his usual siesta and turning up for a conversation—as familiar as bee, butterfly, and breeze.

WHAT BRINGS US
TO PRAYER

FIVE

THE DESIRE FOR LOVE:
"I cannot live with You"

God Is Love

The two great themes of mystical prayer are the desire for love and the fact of death. Both of these drive a person to the limits of existence and are an introduction to the immensity of God. They unlock the hopes and dreams, the longings and fragility of the human heart. It is in mystical prayer that we reach heart level in our seeking and discovery.

Upon his election as pope in 2005, Joseph Ratzinger pondered what would be his inaugural encyclical. He decided it had to be about love, just love. This, he said, is what the Christian faith is about. Now Pope Benedict XVI, he selected for his text this passage from the First Letter of John: "God is love, and he who abides in love abides in God, and God abides in him" (1 John 4:16). At that moment in human history, he writes, religion and violence seem partners in the eradication of unbelief. But even more centrally to Christianity itself, God's love, the pope writes, has been reduced to an abstraction, to something nonhuman or even antihuman and having nothing to do with us.

> More significantly, though, we questioned whether the message of love proclaimed to us by the Bible and the Church's Tradition has some contact with the common human experience of love, or whether it is opposed to that experience. This in turn led us to consider two fundamental words: *eros*, as a term to indicate "worldly" love, and *agape*, referring to love grounded in and shaped by faith. The two notions are often contrasted as "ascending" love and "descending" love. . . . [T]hese distinctions have often been radicalized to the point of establishing a clear antithesis between them: descending, oblative love—*agape*—would be typically Christian while on the other hand ascending, possessive or covetous love—*eros*—would be typical of non-Christian, and particularly Greek culture. Were this antithesis to be taken to extremes, the essence of Christianity would be detached from the vital relations fundamental to human existence, and would become a world apart, admirable perhaps, but decisively cut off from the complex fabric of human life. Yet *eros* and *agape*—ascending and descending love—can never be completely separated. The more the two, in their different aspects, find a proper unity in the one reality of love, the more the true nature of love in general is realized.[1]

Pope Benedict goes on to cite the biblical prophets Hosea and Ezekiel in their descriptions of God manifesting passionate love for us using bold erotic images and metaphors of betrothal and marriage. He continues:

> We can thus see how the reception of the Song of Songs in the canon of sacred Scripture was soon explained by the idea that these love songs ultimately describe God's relation to man and man's relation to God. Thus the Song of Songs became, both in Christian and Jewish literature, a source of mystical knowledge and experience, an expression of the essence of biblical faith: that man can indeed enter into union with God—his primordial aspiration. But this union is no mere fusion, a sinking in a nameless ocean of the Divine; it is a unity which creates love, a unity in which both God and man remain themselves and yet become fully one.[2]

St. John of the Cross (1542–1591) was a recently ordained priest of twenty-five when he met St. Teresa of Ávila, then fifty-two and at the height of her reforming powers. She asked him to be her spiritual director and chaplain of the convents of her reformed Carmelite order. When John later started referring to her as "my daughter," the nuns rebelled. Referring to her *chico*— young in age, short in height—she told them he was "huge" in the eyes of God. His writings of spiritual direction drew heavily upon the Song of Songs, as did Teresa's *Exclamations of the Soul to God*. Inheriting the dry scholastic theology of his day, St. John presents a much broader horizon, one that is not prissy, stale, or exhausted. God is new, daring, and vital. God's whole aim, he teaches, is to make us *grande*. Outside of God everything is narrow.

When God gazes out upon the abyss of nothingness, the result, he says, is creation flamboyant in beauty. It is God who seeks us out and not the reverse. But for God to enter, we have to make a space, a *nada*. John defines asceticism as "clearing away the ground to make way for the miracle of God."[3] When John neared death, his religious brothers began reciting the ritual prayers for the dying, but John checked them: "This is not necessary. Read me something from the Song of Songs."[4]

The Song of Songs is the most cited book of the Old Testament apart from the psalms. Much of it is a dialog between a man and a woman. It begins with the woman's yearning.

> Let him kiss me with kisses of his mouth!
> More delightful is your love than wine!
>
> > Your name spoken is a spreading perfume—
> that is why the maidens love you.
>
> Draw me!—
>
> > We will follow you eagerly!
> > Bring me, O king, to your chambers.
>
> With you we rejoice and exult,
> we extol your love; it is beyond wine:
> how rightly you are loved! (Song 1:1-4)

The coming of spring sparks the flame of love.

> Hark! My lover—here he comes
> > springing across the mountains,
> > leaping across the hills.
> My lover is like a gazelle
> > or a young stag.
> Here he stands behind our wall,
> > gazing through the windows,
> > peering through the lattices.
> My lover speaks; he says to me,
> > "Arise, my beloved, my beautiful one, and come!
> "For see, the winter is past,
> > the rains are over and gone.
> The flowers appear on the earth,
> > the time of pruning the vines has come,
> > and the song of the dove is heard in our land.
> The fig tree puts forth its figs,
> > and the vines, in bloom, give forth fragrance.
> Arise, my beloved, my beautiful one,
> > and come!
>
> "O my dove in the clefts of the rock,
> > in the secret recesses of the cliff,
> Let me see you,
> > let me hear your voice,
> For your voice is sweet,
> > and you are lovely." (Song 2:8-14)

The canticles end with the power of love even over death.

Set me as a seal on your heart,
 as a seal on your arm;
For stern as death is love,
 relentless as the nether world is devotion;
 its flames are a blazing fire.
Deep waters cannot quench love,
 nor floods sweep it away.
Were one to offer all he owns to purchase love,
 he would be roundly mocked. (Song 8:6-7).

This love song, interpreted in both Jewish and Christian traditions as expressing God's seeking of an intimate relationship with the human soul, becomes something entirely different in Emily Dickinson's version of it.

The Heart asks Pleasure - first -
And then - excuse from Pain -
And then - those little Anodynes
That deaden suffering -

And then - to go to sleep -
And then - if it should be
The will of it's Inquisitor
The privilege to die -

(C.P. 588)

In a succession of growing and growing disappointments expressed by the relentless series of "and then," "and then," "and then," and "and then," the human heart that at first innocently and trustingly asks God for the pleasure of his love comes to realize that this "Inquisitor" is totally uninterested in her. As her requests become smaller and smaller, she ends by pleading just for the "privilege" of death, please, please. God, she comes to understand, is actually, to use a phrase from Helen Vendler's interpretation of this most uncomfortable poetic outburst, not her Lover but actually the sadistic Refuser—in fact, her Torturer![5]

Emily Dickinson's Yearning for Love

It is surprising to encounter a frankly erotic poem in Emily Dickinson's corpus. What makes this poem all the more impressive is that the poet is imaging something, were it to happen, that would satisfy her wildest desires—but it never actually took place.

> Wild nights - Wild nights!
> Were it with thee
> Wild nights should be
> Our luxury!
>
> Futile - the winds -
> To a Heart in port -
> Done with the Compass -
> Done with the Chart!

Rowing in Eden -
Ah - the Sea!
Might I but moor - tonight -
In thee!

(C.P. 269)

In the prevailing religious and social climate of New England, Emily Dickinson came to the conviction expressed in many poems that she would never receive the love her heart was seeking. She was taught that human nature was depraved, its deepest aspirations untrustworthy. God, the remote and eternal arbiter of human fate, was coldly indifferent to the cruelty of human existence. And so she developed within herself the strength to defy God, to dethrone God and replace him.

In a poem among her greatest, Dickinson addresses the human lover with whom she wishes to live forever, for without him God's Paradise would be a "sordid excellence"—beneath contempt, filthy. Her greatest fear is that she and he could never become united because he was a believer and she an unbelieving outcast. Their meeting in the end happens in a place of her own creation—the poem we are now reading.

I cannot live with You -
It would be Life -
And Life is over there -
Behind the Shelf

The Sexton keeps the key to -
Putting up
Our Life - His Porcelain -
Like a Cup -

Discarded of the Housewife -
Quaint - or Broke -
A newer Sevres pleases -
Old Ones crack –

I could not die - with You -
For One must wait
To shut the Other's Gaze down -
You - could not -

And I - Could I stand by
And see you - freeze -
Without my Right of Frost -
Death's privilege?

Nor could I rise - with You -
Because Your Face
Would put out Jesus' -
That New Grace

Glow plain - and foreign
On my homesick eye -
Except that You than He
Shone closer by -

They'd judge Us - How -
For You - served Heaven - You know,

Or sought to -
I could not -

Because You saturated sight
And I had no more eyes
For sordid excellence
As Paradise

And were You lost, I would be -
Though my name
Rang loudest
On the Heavenly fame -

And were You - saved -
And I - condemned to be
Where You were not -
That self - were Hell to me-

So we must meet apart -
You there - I - here -
With just the Door ajar
That Oceans are - and Prayer -
And that White Sustenance -
Despair -

(C.P. 706)

In this extraordinary poem—extraordinary for its length
but especially because of its emotional intensity—
Dickinson unveils her inner turmoil nearing despair.
She has lost all perspective, obsessing over her lover
and their future together. Everything else is secondary,

even God. She cares about nothing else, not personal fame, not Heaven or Hell.

Her list of disappointments is large. The first she mentions is the sacrament of the Holy Eucharist, Christ's promise of eternal life through the reception of his Body and Blood. God, referred to in the poem as the Sexton and later as an ordinary Housewife, has locked the chalice up in the church sacristy or discarded it as quaint and cracked. Reading these lines we recall that in the Protestantism then prevailing, the celebration of Holy Communion was infrequent, Sunday worship consisting of Bible reading, sermons, and hymns. The Eucharist, or some attenuated form of it, was a holdover from the discarded Catholic tradition. There was no Real Presence of Christ, just a memorial of something irretrievably in the past. Grape juice was the substitute for wine. When the infrequent communion service took place, only publicly professed believers were allowed to participate—certainly not a person like Emily Dickinson. The poem's last lines return to a eucharistic reference: "that White Sustenance," which no longer signifies salvation but "Despair," the poem's final word.

Teresa of Ávila with her Jewish parentage always felt the need to defend the orthodoxy of her faith by inserting trinitarian language into her mystical treatises. The Spanish Inquisition was constantly looking over her shoulder. This did not mean, however, that her personal experiences of the ineffable God and God's love could not be conveyed through the images she created. I see something of the same dynamic in Emily Dickinson's mystical poetry, including in the poem we are analyzing here. But she had to reject the God of her culture as a caricature of her personal religious experience, which Teresa did not find it necessary to do.

When Dickinson speaks of God, it has to be in terms that are real and authentic. Nature, it turns out, is a revelation and an encounter with God's Real and True Presence. This she describes magnificently in one of her most famous poems.

> Further in Summer than the Birds -
> Pathetic from the Grass -
> A minor Nation celebrates
> It's unobtrusive Mass.
>
> No Ordinance be seen -
> So gradual the Grace
> A gentle Custom it becomes -
> Enlarging Loneliness -
>
> Antiquest felt at Noon -
> When August burning low
> Arise this spectral Canticle
> Repose to typify -
>
> Remit as yet no Grace -
> No furrow on the Glow,
> But a Druidic Difference
> Enhances Nature now -
>
> (C.P. 895)

In the magnificent array of nature that is cherished in the New England summer, Dickinson hears a humble chorus of beetles arriving late in the season and celebrating what she perceives to be a Mass. Dickinson collected beetles and preserved them as gifts. Did she see herself as such a humble beetle and her poetry part of their chorus? Beetles are so inconsequential, yet she hears in their chirping the enactment of a religious ritual, a "gentle Custom" that becomes an enlarging "Grace." They announce through their religious canticle, like the liturgical Benedictus and Magnificat, the coming of fall and the Sabbath repose. Nature itself is enhanced by the "Difference" they announce. The progress of the sacred ceremony they enact is gradual and unfolding, revealing the infinite bounds of our loneliness, the empty space, the nothingness, the *nada* of St. John of the Cross, for God's presence to fill as autumn draws near. Nature now is no longer nature, for it is enhanced by what theologians call "sacramental consciousness." This sacramental consciousness opens us beyond present existence to ultimate reality. As Richard Wilbur comments regarding Dickinson's poetic vision, "Therefore her nature poetry, when most serious, does not play descriptively with birds or flowers but presents us repeatedly with dawn, noon and sunset, those grand ceremonial moments of the day that argue the splendor of Paradise."[6]

The sacraments rely on basic human realities to represent and communicate divine realities: bread and wine, water and oil, human words and human touch. Through nature's sacrament Emily Dickinson and God are meeting at last in a relationship of love.

SIX

THE FEAR OF DEATH:
"Safe in their Alabaster Chambers"

The Christian Belief in Everlasting Life

The Congregational Church of Amherst, in which the Dickinson family was so prominent, professed like most Christians the ancient statements of faith. The final articles of the Apostles' Creed, from the early second century, profess: "I believe in the Holy Spirit, the holy catholic church, the communion of saints, the forgiveness of sins, the resurrection of the body, and life everlasting." The doctrines of resurrection and life eternal had special meaning in nineteenth-century Amherst because it was the era of one of the bloodiest wars in human history, the American Civil War, and also because death was such a fixation in the general culture.

It is only in the second creation account in the book of Genesis that the phenomenon of death is introduced,

and there as a colossal aberration from the divine inten-
tion in creating the garden paradise of earth. God took
the risk of endowing human beings uniquely with the
gift of freedom, with tragic consequences both for them
and for the rest of creation entrusted to their care. Death
enters, but only gradually as the gift of immortality is
withdrawn from successive generations. The first re-
corded death in human history in fact was a murder,
Cain's murder of his brother Abel (Gen 4:8). As St. Paul
would comment much later, in the Letter to the Romans,
death is not a natural phenomenon in Christian theology
but is "the wages of sin" (Rom 6:23). Jesus, God's Son,
in solidarity with us underwent death himself, and God
raised him up again "so that he could become the first-
fruits of those who have fallen asleep" (1 Cor 15:20), for
God "is not God of the dead but of the living" (Mark
12:27).

We now live in that interim period between the res-
urrection of Christ and the general resurrection of all
humanity. In his Letter to the Philippians, St. Paul writes,
"Our citizenship is in heaven, and from it we await a
savior, the Lord Jesus Christ. He will change our lowly
bodies to conform with his glorified body by the power
that enables him also to bring all things into subjection
to himself" (Phil 3:20-21). All of creation is destined
therefore to share in this resurrection (Rom 8:19-23),
when there will be "a new heaven and a new earth"
(Rev 21:1).

The general resurrection is when the promised Last Judgment takes place, when Christ returns as the judge of the righteous and the unrighteous (Acts 24:15). All then must render an account before him and receive their eternal destiny.

At the end of his encyclical letter *Laudato Si'* (*On Care for Our Common Home*), Pope Francis reflects upon this glorious destiny after all the triumphs and tragedies of human history, personal and cosmic.

> At the end, we will find ourselves face to face with the infinite beauty of God (1 Cor 13:12), and be able to read with admiration and happiness the mystery of the universe, which with us will share in unending plenitude. Even now we are journeying towards the sabbath of eternity, the new Jerusalem, towards our common home in heaven. Jesus says: "I make all things new" (Rev 21:5). Eternal life will be a shared experience of awe, in which every creature, resplendently transfigured, will take its rightful place and have something to give those poor men and women who will have been liberated once and for all.[1]

Emily Dickinson's Preoccupation with Death

A major theme in Emily Dickinson's mystical poetry is the fact of death and her fear of personal extinction. From her windows overlooking Main Street she looked down routinely on funeral processions to West Cemetery, just around the corner, where she herself would eventually be interred. Deaths of her loved ones only multiplied as her solitary life became more and more impoverished. As we have noted, her father died in June 1874. One year later her mother had the crippling stroke that led to her death seven years later; Emily was her principal caregiver during those seven years. Samuel Bowles, Emily's mentor and senior by only four years, died in 1878 at the age of fifty-one. Her closest personal male friend, Charles Wadsworth, died in April 1882. On April 5, 1883, her young nephew Gilbert, who lived next door, also tragically passed away. But even amid such personal bereavement as she moved toward her own death in 1886 after nearly two years of being confined to bed, Emily's spiritual struggles with death eased and her encounters with God became more familial and intimate.

But not until those last years . . . In one of her early poems most familiar to young and old, she describes death coming to meet her in terms of an extraterrestrial chariot ride. When I was teaching elementary schoolchildren, I recall, this was one of their favorites. Little did they understand its underlying deception, disillusion, and despair.

> Because I could not stop for Death -
> He kindly stopped for me -
> The Carriage held but just Ourselves -
> And Immortality.

We slowly drove - He knew no haste
And I had put away
My labor and my leisure too,
For his Civility -

We passed the School, where Children strove
At Recess - in the Ring -
We passed the Fields of Gazing Grain -
We passed the Setting Sun -

Or rather - He passed Us -
The Dews drew quivering and Chill -
For only Gossamer, my Gown -
My Tippet - only Tulle -

We paused before a House that seemed
A Swelling of the Ground -
The Roof was scarcely visible -
The Cornice - in the Ground -

Since then - 'tis Centuries - and yet
Feels shorter than the Day
I first surmised the Horses' Heads
Were toward Eternity -

(C.P. 479)

As the poet contemplates her own death, death appears as a friendly companion offering her transition from earthly existence to personal immortality. Death here is more like "Sister Death" in the "Canticle of the Creatures" of St. Francis of Assisi. But then the journey becomes less comfortable when it dawns on her where they are heading. No longer warm because the sun has set, she finds her skimpy summer clothes poor protection in the growing cold and dark. She notices below a grave—her own future dwelling?—that is sinking in the ground, her final dissolution. Her naïve belief in personal immortality is shattered when she surmises where she is now heading: not to immortality but to an empty "Eternity."

In another famous reflection on death, the poet interrupts the solemn moment with the trivial detail of a fly buzz as the last thing she hears.

I heard a Fly buzz - when I died -
The Stillness in the Room
Was like the Stillness in the Air -
Between the Heaves of Storm -

The Eyes around - had wrung them dry -
And Breaths were gathering firm
For that last Onset - when the King
Be witnessed - in the Room -

I willed my Keepsakes - Signed away
What portion of me be
Assignable - and then it was
There interposed a Fly -

With Blue - uncertain - stumbling Buzz -
Between the light - and me -

And then the Windows failed - and then
I could not see to see -

(C.P. 591)

The last sense to leave us when we die is reported to be
the ability to hear. But when the poet is dying, the sound
she hears is not consoling—it is the blue, uncertain,
stumbling buzz of an ordinary fly, one of the flies that
customarily gather around a decaying corpse. She was
anticipating something else as her life's conclusion—the
King in the Room—but instead comes this fly at the end,
not even the butterfly St. Teresa of Ávila imagined to
symbolize her soul's beauty and immortality. Her final
dissolution is portrayed in a rapid series of "and then,"
"and then," "and then." In place of hymns of angels her
last memory is of a pedestrian buzzing fly, representing
her total extinction.

One of the only eleven poems published during
Dickinson's lifetime was also devoted to the theme of
death. Disguised with traditional Christian imagery, the
poem conveys the finality of death.

Safe in their Alabaster Chambers -
Untouched by Morning -
And untouched by noon -
Sleep the meek members of the Resurrection -
Rafter of Satin and Roof of Stone -

Grand go the Years,
In the Crescent above them -
Worlds scoop their Arcs -
And Firmaments - row -
Diadems - drop -
And Doges - surrender -
Soundless as Dots,
On a Disc of Snow.

(C.P. 124)

The poet has the meek believers in the resurrection put away as safely as in a bank's safe deposit box, inert and untouched. Some safety! In the second stanza the scene shifts from the earthly to the cosmic. In such a perspective the earth and all its inhabitants fade into total insignificance. Eternity's grand passage, the infinite constellations reduce these once-powerful figures to mere dots. The poem's relentless repetition of *d*s underscores the point: diadems drop, doges as dots, everything on a fragile disc of quickly melting snow.

Dickinson described her poetry as a wrestling with God like the biblical patriarch Jacob's wrestling with a mysterious "man" at Peniel. The "man" turns out to be God, but because Jacob is the better wrestler, God has to wound Jacob to escape his hold. Before returning to heaven God confers upon the limping Jacob the blessing he had asked for and also a new name, "Israel," meaning "one who has struggled with God" (Gen 32:25-31). The fear of extinction and the divine deception of a promise of immortality were central to Dickinson's struggles with God, until, as we have seen, her growing appreciation of the doctrine of the incarnation of God as human in Christ made being human something less tragic and God far less remote and uncaring. The sacramental presence of God in creation, along with the divine plan of redemption in Christ, took away fear at last.

In a letter to Thomas Higginson, Dickinson suggested that "the supernatural is only the natural disclosed."[2] This profound insight put into question the two-layered religious conception of reality as natural and supernatural, with nothing but an arbitrary connection between them. To correct this erroneous view, Karl Rahner, much later in Catholic theology, would speak of the "supernatural existential." Pure nature, he argues, never existed except as an abstract philosophical concept. Historical nature as created by God from the beginning was ordered and open to the supernatural. "Man," he writes, "should be able to receive this Love which is God himself; he must have a congeniality for it. He must be able to accept it . . . as one who has room and scope, understanding and desire for it. He must have a real potency for it. He must have it always. He is indeed someone always addressed and claimed by this Love. For, as he now in fact is, he is created for it; he is thought and called into being so that Love might bestow itself."[3] In other words, again following Rahner, the experience of the self is the experience of God. Our "supernatural existential," the only existence that is, is our God-given orientation to holy mystery.

CONCLUSION:
"My Business is Circumference"

St. Teresa of Ávila (1515–1582) and
Emily Dickinson

Nearing the age of fifty, Teresa of Ávila at the direction of her male spiritual advisors wrote her autobiography, *La vida* (*The Life*). She began writing it between other chores in 1562 and completed it in 1565. In it she describes her experience of mystical prayer. She is also discovering herself.

> When picturing Christ in the way I have mentioned, and sometimes even when reading, I used unexpectedly to experience a consciousness of the presence of God of such a kind that I could not possibly doubt that he was within me or that I was totally engulfed in him. This was in no sense a vision: I believe it is called mystical theology. The soul is suspended in such a way that it seems to be completely outside itself. The will loves; the memory, I think, is almost lost; while the understanding, I believe, though it is not lost, does not

> reason—I mean that it does not work, but is amazed
> at the extent of all it can understand; for God wills it
> to realize that it understands nothing of what His
> Majesty represents to it.[1]

Teresa entered the convent at age sixteen and there experienced twenty years of restlessness and disillusion. Religious life in the convent was a refuge for unmarried women supported by the dowries their families provided. It lacked discipline and focus. After twenty years of this, and having endured many health issues both physical and mental as a result, in 1554 Teresa began having the first of her mystical visions leading to what she described as her "conversion." Her creative powers were unleashed. It came to her that it was the Carmelite order itself that needed reform. She reformed the order as she had hoped and went on to found seventeen convents of the Discalced Carmelites. She also began to write.

In addition to *Vida* and many other compositions, she gifted the nuns with another masterpiece, *Las moradas* (*Interior Castle*), written between 1577 and 1578, which we have cited earlier. Using her imagination to find images for what she was experiencing, she demonstrated that mysticism is an experimental science. And yet she was always aware that she was stealing time from other pressing tasks like her spinning. Writing was a kind of therapy. She was refounding a religious order and refounding herself at the same time.

In *Vida* she resorts to our experience of water making our garden grow to explain the progress of prayer. She asks us to imagine water irrigating the garden of our soul in four stages, from where we do all the hard work cranking it out of the ground, through the hard spiritual work of repentance for our transgressions and the practice of solitude, before we find ourselves totally immersed as in a stream or river where we can float in the arms of God. Then the rain comes down on us and we experience rapture. Her ultimate lesson in *Vida* for the nuns is "Be merry, my daughters!"[2] She wants them to realize ultimately that it is foolish to think we can enter heaven without knowing ourselves.[3]

During Madre's lifetime, St. Augustine's *Confessions*, regarded as the first autobiography ever written, was translated into Spanish. Ten years after his conversion to Christianity and now the bishop of Hippo, Augustine asked what real change he could notice in himself. He found that in most ways he was the same person he had been before. What he could testify ("testimony" being the meaning of *confessions*—a testimony to the effects within him of divine grace) was that he was more comfortable with himself, more tranquil about his virtues and his vices. He could actually like himself! He testifies to God, "Behold, you were in me and I was outside myself. I sought myself in things outside of me and found beauty in them and not in myself. You were with me all the time; the problem was I was not with you."[4]

In *Interior Castle*, Teresa counsels that we should not spend too much time in the first three mansions on the periphery where we are striving to overcome our faults through the serious work of repentance. As soon as you can, she says, move to the fourth mansion, the quiet room where the Holy Spirit is waiting. There you can let the Holy Spirit do all the work. To describe the transformation that takes place there she summons the image of the silkworm, large and ugly in its tight cocoon, that emerges and discovers itself a beautiful, white butterfly.[5] The soul is now so gorgeous it can't even recognize itself! Christ himself, amazingly, has found you a worthy dwelling to live in.

Interior Castle was translated into English in 1675. Perhaps it was the inspiration for a poem of Emily Dickinson's describing herself as that butterfly. We do know that Dickinson had on the wall of her upstairs room framed pictures of Elizabeth Barrett Browning and George Eliot. She greatly admired Eliot's *Middlemarch*, written during the years 1871–1872, calling it "glory." The novel begins with the author's testimony to the inspiration of Teresa of Ávila.

Who that cares much to know the history of man, and how the mysterious mixture behaves under the varying experiments of Time, has not dwelt, at least briefly, on the life of St. Theresa, has not smiled with some gentleness at the thought of the little girl walking forth one morning hand-in-hand with her still smaller brother, to go and seek martyrdom in the country of the Moors? Out they toddled from rugged Avila, wide-eyed and helpless looking as two fawns, but with human hearts, already beating to a national idea; until domestic reality met them in the shape of uncles and turned them back from their great resolve. That child-pilgrimage was a fit beginning. Theresa's passionate, ideal nature demanded an epic life: what were many-volumed romances of chivalry and the social conquests of a brilliant girl to her? Her flame quickly burned up that light fuel; and, fed from within, soared after some illimitable satisfaction, some object which would never justify weariness, which would reconcile self-despair with the rapturous consciousness of life beyond self. She found her epos in the reform of a religious order.

That Spanish woman who lived three hundred years ago was certainly not the last of her kind. Many Theresas have been born who found for themselves no epic life wherein there was a constant unfolding of far-resonant action; perhaps only a life of mistakes, the offspring of a certain spiritual grandeur ill-matched with the meanness of opportunity; perhaps a tragic failure which found no sacred poet and sank unwept into oblivion. With dim lights and tangled circumstance they tried to shape their thought and deed in noble agreement; but after all, to common eyes their struggles seemed mere inconsistency and formlessness; for these later-born Theresas were helped by no

coherent social faith and order which could perform
the function of knowledge for the ardently willing
soul. Their ardour alternated between a vague ideal
and the common yearning of womanhood; so that the
one was disapproved as extravagance, and the other
condemned as a lapse.[6]

It is not difficult to understand why Emily Dickinson
would identify herself with such a figure.

> My Cocoon tightens - Colors teaze -
> I'm feeling for the Air -
> A dim capacity for Wings
> Demeans the dress I wear -
>
> A power of Butterfly must be -
> The Aptitude to fly
> Meadows of Majesty concedes
> And easy Sweeps of Sky -
>
> So I must baffle at the Hint
> And cipher at the Sign
> And make much blunder, if at last
> I take the clue divine -
>
> (C.P. 1107)

Avila and Amherst

The fortified hilltop town of Avila has its origin over
a thousand years ago. Nine gates penetrate its medieval

walls, from which rise eighty-eight towers surveying the surrounding plain. Avila provided Madre Teresa with the landscape to give form to her mystical visions.

> As soon as you step inside the walls, you realize that the fortified space of the saint's home city is the model for her *moradas* or Dwelling Places, misleadingly named *The Interior Castle*, as she described them late in life, in 1577, at the request of her friend and confessor Jerome Gratian. The *moradas* could not have been conceived without the *Hekhalot* and Avila: a haphazard agglomeration of little houses, plazas, and barrios, partitioned off from one another and yet open and permeable. By the monumental grace of those eighty-eight towers that bulge and snake rhythmically around the holy of holies, the *moradas* or "abodes" of Avila communicate with one another just as they do with the mountains, fields, and sky. Avila "expands in its smallness" as an effect of those walls, wrote Miguel de Unamuno. No, Avila is in no sense "small," because all of its boundaries are membranes. Instead of enclosing and compacting it, that great concertina of a wall inflates and transcends it. Here, every indoors is half-way to being outdoors; Avila streams with greatness.[7]

Emily Dickinson is incomprehensible apart from the town of Amherst. Within its particular landscape, its weathers and seasons, she experienced the mystical presence—or absence—of God that became her poetry, "A Music numerous as space - / But neighboring as Noon -" (C.P. 504).

> Because I see - New Englandly -
> The Queen, discerns like me -
> Provincially -

(C.P. 256)

As we have earlier mentioned, "Standing in Amherst, Emily Dickinson could look into the heart of Eternity."[8]

Teresa grew up in a house with eight male siblings and with the unspoken impression of male superiority. The convent was one of the few available means of escape from male dominance for this woman who often came across to persons of authority as rebellious and headstrong. In her *Way of Perfection*, she instructs the nuns, "I would not want you, my daughters, to be womanish in anything, nor would I want you to be like women but like strong men."[9] Her reformed Carmelite order was to be for an elite of robust constitution.

Emily Dickinson's father and brother were prominent lawyers, leaders in the local Congregational church and at Amherst College. What would a virginal spinster like Emily, living her life in seclusion in this provincial town, be expected to know about anything? Known to all as "the Squire," the "Father of the House" was given due deference from his family—except, on occasion, from Emily. Her niece recalls, "Aunt Lavinia used to tell how once, when some message of his to the man about the frogs in the lower meadow had not been executed with becoming dispatch, their father took his hat and cane in high dudgeon, and walked out, remarking haughtily, 'I'll speak to the frogs myself about it!'—too vexed to notice his absurd slip of the tongue, and was met by Emily on his return with, 'Did you find the frogs deferential, Father?' "[10] The niece also makes this observation: "Between the abrupt ending of school routine and the fatal hour of marriage there was for every girl a chasm to be filled in. Emily's imagination and intuition were to reject the local program. That she was capable of her own decision in her own time was to be exactly the proof of her genius."[11]

It is not surprising that both these exceptional women endured extended periods of despondency and psychosomatic illness until they discovered themselves beyond the restrictions of prevailing religious and social norms. In *Life*, Teresa remembers her first twenty years in the convent as a great trial. "One needs to be careful," she continues, "women especially so, since we are very weak and may come to great harm if we are told in so many words that we are deluded by the devil."[12] But once they came into their own, there was no stopping them!

Teresa's two masterpieces, *Vida* and *Las moradas*, written, it is true, at the instruction of her male spiritual directors, were creative outbursts, both full of "sweet disorder," numerous parentheses, transpositions, random asides, and homespun metaphors that just occurred to her. In a similar way, Dickinson's "poems," as they came to be known, were jotted down in her idio-syncratic style—numerous dashes between words, unusual capitalizations, her handwriting described as resembling fossilized bird tracks. Hundreds of such poems poured out in her most productive years. Dickinson often wrote on the run, using any material at hand: commercial advertisements, newspaper clippings, pieces of fabric, pressed flowers, dead bugs, used envelopes.

Teresa is remembered today as the great saint of the Catholic Counter-Reformation and of Baroque piety. In an atmosphere calling for a return to religious conformity enforced by the Inquisition, she insisted upon the authenticity of personal religious experience. The humanity of Christ, which was one with his divinity, made being human, along with human emotion and piety, acceptable. We find these powerful religious sentiments inspiring the contemporary Spanish Baroque artists Zurbarán, Velasquez, and Murillo. In a similar manner Emily Dickinson's poetry is in part a corrective to the coercive religious revivalism of her time.

In 2015, the five-hundredth anniversary of the birth of Teresa of Ávila, I made a pilgrimage to Avila with two of my classmates, one a cardinal, the other an archbishop. We were given a warm welcome by the sisters of the Convent of St. Joseph founded by Teresa.

We offered Mass with the sisters singing from their enclosure in a balcony above the sanctuary. They excitedly invited us inside the cloister and spoke of Madre as if she were in the next room. "Madre always wanted us to keep busy," one explained to me, "so that we do not become too introspective." I expressed to this nun my surprise that Madre's particular cell, which is located right next to the altar, had in addition to a bed, table, and trunk a private kitchen. "Oh," she explained, "that was before her reform!"

Very often over the years I have visited the Dickinson Homestead in Amherst and the Evergreens next door, home of Emily's brother, Austin, and his wife, Susan. Each year, it seems, work is being done to restore the property, now under the direction of Amherst College, to its original state. Emily's conservatory received reconstruction in 2017. A tour guide takes groups through, the highlight being her second-floor bedroom. In addition to the Franklin stove and her narrow sleigh bed, there are replicas of the bureau in which her poems were discovered after her death and the square writing table and small chair next to it (the originals are preserved at the Houghton Library of Harvard University). Also on display is a copy of Emily's special white dress. In this room, its large windows looking down on one side to Main Street where she could observe the arrival of any visitor, and on the other across the trees to the Evergreens, Emily lived and died—her cloister.

Should Madre Teresa and Emily Dickinson meet in eternity, the encounter would have to be electric: two highly intelligent, bookish, passionate women, at times funny and satirical, who changed the world in which they lived and the world thereafter. The boundless energy of Madre Teresa, whose life has been characterized as a long and difficult journey on bumpy roads, and Dickinson's whole creative oeuvre hidden away in a bureau drawer for another generation to discover— both manifest a powerful if unexpressed surety and self-confidence. Yet they both saw their individual lives as a small part of an enormous and barely glimpsed project. As Teresa put it, "Let nothing disturb you, nothing dismay you. All things are passing, God never changes. Patient endurance attains all things. God alone suffices."

Emily Dickinson's Way to Heaven

We have described Emily Dickinson's religious situation as "believing unbelief." Her Puritan heritage was too constrictive and negative to accommodate the capaciousness of her searching mind and rich internal experience. Her poem "The World is not conclusion," written in her early thirties at the beginning of her most intense poetic outburst, begins with twelve lines that more or less set forth the foundations for a Puritan belief; the last eight undermine them. The supernatural must exist somewhere, but alas, so far as we can discern, not here.

This World is not conclusion.
A Species stands beyond -
Invisible, as Music -
But positive, as Sound -
It beckons, and it baffles -
Philosophy, dont know -
And through a Riddle, at the last -
Sagacity, must go -
To guess it, puzzles scholars -
To gain it, Men have borne
Contempt of Generations
And Crucifixion, shown -
Faith slips - and laughs, and rallies -
Blushes, if any see -
Plucks at a twig of Evidence -
And asks a Vane, the way -
Much Gesture, from the Pulpit -
Strong Hallelujahs roll -
Narcotics cannot still the Tooth
That nibbles at the soul -

(C.P. 373)

The poem begins with the firm religious belief that the world we know is not all that is. The next line originally began "A Sequel stands beyond," which Dickinson revised to read "A Species . . . ," perhaps a reference to Darwin's *On the Origin of Species*, then under discussion? Philosophy can take us only so far, and religious figures

like Jesus, who witnessed to this belief by suffering cru-
cifixion, must bear the weight. Faith seeks any reassur-
ance, even the changing direction of the weather vane
atop Congregational churches. Sermons and hymns
seem more like narcotics to remove the pain of unbelief,
the "Tooth," not the "Truth" that keeps nibbling.

Emily Dickinson once tried to comfort a friend who
had suffered a severe loss. She said, "I cannot pray, but
I can sing." Her song was poetry, a form of mystical
prayer through which she sought to find the "center"
by exploring its vast "circumference."

> Circumference thou Bride of Awe
> Possessing thou shalt be
> Possessed by every hallowed Knight
> That dares - to Covet thee

(C.P. 1636)

Richard Sewall in his two-volume biography of the poet
quotes her as saying, "The Bible dealt with the Centre,
not with the Circumference." He comments, "Earlier
she had stated her own 'business' as Circumference by
which she probably meant (in 1862) her purpose was to
encompass the truth of life, the whole range of human
experience, and somehow to arrest it in poetry. She set
out to be Expositor, Interpreter, Analyst, Orpheus—all
in one."[13]

In a convulsive poem, from 1863, Dickinson careens from metaphor to metaphor to explain her exploration of outer space, of Circumference, and her feeling of dis-equilibrium and ultimate loneliness.

> I saw no Way - The Heavens were stitched -
> I felt the Columns close -
> The Earth reversed her Hemispheres -
> I touched the Universe -
>
> And back it slid - and I alone -
> A speck upon a Ball -
> Went out upon Circumference -
> Beyond the Dip of Bell -
>
> (C.P. 633)

She has lost her way. Heaven is "stitched," its door columns closed. She is describing what St. John of the Cross knew as the *nada*, utter emptiness. She goes from feeling herself just "a speck upon a Ball" to being "beyond the Dip of Bell," which is totally incoherent. And yet she reports that in the process "I touched the Universe," the vastness of Circumference. Nicholas of Cusa (1401–1464), the late medieval theologian, wrote about such a mystical experience of the divine presence—and absence. God, he says, "is the Being whose center is everywhere and whose circumference is nowhere."[14] In addition, Dickinson's mystical vision was seeking to overcome the theologically artificial and unsupportable separation of God from the world that she inherited from her Puritan heritage. Pope Benedict XVI has enlightening words on this subject from the Catholic perspective.

> Because there is not somewhere, a place where God sits, God is the place beyond all places. If you look into the world, you do not see heaven, but you see traces of God everywhere. In the structure of matter, in all the rationality of reality. Even when you see human beings, you find traces of God. You see vices but you also see goodness and love. These are the places where God is.[15]

Speaking to the Athenians and trying to bridge the gap between their conceptions of God and Christianity, St. Paul in similar fashion tried to explain what they termed the "Unknown God."

> He made from one the whole human race to dwell on the entire surface of the earth, and he fixed the ordered seasons and the boundaries of their regions, so that people might seek God, even perhaps grope for him and find him, though indeed he is not far from any one of us. For "In him we live and move and have our being," as even some of your poets have said, "For we too are his offspring." Since therefore we are the offspring of God, we ought not to think that the divinity

is like an image fashioned from gold, silver, or stone by human art and imagination. (Acts 17:26-29)

The mature Emily Dickinson, as we have seen, constructed for herself a new persona as an authoritative interpreter of the world. But as she gets out of her own depth and falls into the vastness of what she calls "Circumference," she begins to experience what St. Paul described as the passage from the "I" to the "no longer I," the discovery of her true self as more beautiful and capacious than she could ever have imagined: "yet I live, no longer I, but Christ lives in me"—"a new creation" (Gal 2:20; 6:15).

In a homily, Pope Benedict XVI speaks of the dislocation and confusing tumble into the Infinite that is what Dickinson refers to as her journey into Circumference.

This liberation of our "I" from its isolation, this finding oneself in a new subject, means finding oneself within the vastness of God and being drawn into a life which has now moved out of the context of "dying and becoming." . . . To live one's own life as continual entry into this open space: this is the meaning of being a Christian.[16]

Wallace Stevens resonates Emily Dickinson in many of his famous poems—"The Snow Man," for example, and "The Auroras of Autumn," to mention another. In

"Of Mere Being," a poem published only after his death, we find a firm echo of Dickinson's stunning poem that begins " 'Hope' is the thing with feathers." Both poems catapult us into the immensity of what Dickinson called Circumference. Both point to the mysterious, all-pervasive presence and perspective of the Holy Spirit.

> "Hope" is the thing with feathers -
> That perches in the soul -
> And sings the tune without the words -
> And never stops - at all -
>
> And sweetest - in the Gale - is heard -
> And sore must be the storm -
> That could abash the little Bird
> That kept so many warm -
>
> I've heard it in the chillest land -
> And on the strangest Sea -
> Yet - never - in Extremity,
> It asked a crumb - of me.
>
> (C.P. 314)

OF MERE BEING

> The palm at the end of the mind,
> Beyond the last thought, rises
> In the bronze decor,

A gold-feathered bird
Sings in the palm, without human meaning,
Without human feeling, a foreign song.

You know that it is not the reason
That makes us happy or unhappy.
The bird sings. Its feathers shine.

The palm stands on the edge of space.
The wind moves slowly in the branches.
The bird's fire-fangled feathers dangle down.[17]

In a poem we cited earlier, Emily Dickinson eventually experienced such personal transformation in her own life.

The Soul should always stand ajar
That if the Heaven inquire
He will not be obliged to wait

(C.P. 1017)

St. Catherine of Siena (1347–1380) famously said, "All the way to heaven is heaven, because Jesus said, 'I am the way.'"[18] To which Emily Dickinson replies,

So instead of getting to Heaven, at last -
I'm going, all along.

(C.P. 236)

NOTES

Texts of Emily Dickinson's poems are from *The Poems of Emily Dickinson*, ed. R. W. Franklin (Cambridge, MA: The Belknap Press of Harvard University Press, 1999).

INTRODUCTION

1. Cynthia Griffin Wolff, *Emily Dickinson* (New York: Alfred A. Knopf, 1986), 535.

2. Virginia Jackson, *Dickinson's Misery: A Theory of Lyric Reading* (Princeton: Princeton University Press, 2005), 204.

3. Ibid., 16.

4. Ibid., 16, 126.

5. Holland Cotter, "Belle of Amherst? Make that Rebel," *New York Times* (January 20, 2017): C15.

6. Michael Kelly, Marta L. Werner, Carolyn Vega, Susan Howe, and Richard Wilbur, *The Networked Recluse: The Connected World of Emily Dickinson* (Amherst, MA: Amherst College Press, 2017), 2.

7. Langdon Hammer, "Inside & Underneath Words," *New York Review of Books* 64, no. 14 (September 28, 2017): 31.

8. Martha Dickinson Bianchi, *Emily Dickinson: Face to Face* (Boston: Houghton Mifflin, 1932), 28.

9. Ibid., 56.

10. Stephanie Merry, "Cynthia Nixon Is Masterful as Emily Dickinson," *Miami Herald* (May 12, 2017).

11. Lawrence Foster, *A Certain Slant of Light: Songs on Poems by Emily Dickinson*, Lisa Delan, Orchestre Philharmonique de Marseille (Baarn, Netherlands: Pentatone, 2018).

ONE: PRAYING MYSTICALLY

1. Augustine, *The Confessions*, trans. John K. Ryan (New York: Doubleday Image, 1960), 133.

2. Origen, *The Song of Songs: Commentary and Homilies*, trans. R. P. Lawson (New York: Newman Press, 1956), 280.

3. Ibid., 198–99.

4. Geoffrey Powell, Kenneth Stevenson, and Rowan Williams, comps., *Love's Redeeming Work: The Anglican Quest for Holiness* (Oxford: Oxford University Press, 2001), 570–71.

5. Augustine, "On the Psalms," quoted in Ivan Nicoletto, *Journey of Faith, Journey of the Universe* (Collegeville, MN: Liturgical Press, 2015), 118.

6. Gregory of Nyssa, *The Life of Moses*, trans. Abraham J. Malherve and Everett Fergusson (New York: Paulist Press, 1978), nos. 225–27.

7. Thérèse of Lisieux, *Story of a Soul*, trans. John Clarke (Washington, DC: ICS Publications, 1996), 213.

8. Mother Teresa, *Come Be My Light*, ed. Brian Kolodiejchuk (New York: Image, 2007), 192–93.

9. Karl Rahner, "Christian Living Formerly and Today," *Theological Investigations* (New York: Herder & Herder, 1971) 7:8.

10. James Wiseman, "Mysticism," in *The New Dictionary of Catholic Spirituality*, ed. Michael Davis (Collegeville, MN: Liturgical Press, 1993), 687.

11. Thérèse of Lisieux, *Story of a Soul*, 242.

12. Teresa of Ávila, *Life*, in *The Complete Works of Saint Teresa of Jesus*, trans. E. Allison Peers (New York: Sheed & Ward, 1944), 1:50.

13. Cynthia Griffin Wolff, *Emily Dickinson* (New York: Alfred A. Knopf, 1986), 468.

14. *The Complete Poems of Emily Dickinson*, Thomas H. Johnson, ed. (Boston: Little, Brown and Company, 1960), 1072.

15. Helen Vendler, *Dickinson: Selected Poems and Commentary* (Cambridge, MA: Harvard University Press, 2010), 603.

16. See Wolff, *Emily Dickinson*, 139ff.

TWO: SOLITUDE

1. Teresa of Ávila, *Interior Castle*, trans. and ed. E. Allison Peers (New York: Doubleday Image, 1988), 36.

2. Ibid., 37.

3. Ibid., 41.

4. Thomas Merton, *Thoughts in Solitude* (Boston: Shambhala, 1993), x–xii.

5. Thomas Merton, *No Man Is an Island* (New York: Harcourt Brace, 1955), 228.

6. Teresa of Ávila, *Interior Castle*, 32–33.

7. Helen Vendler, *Dickinson: Selected Poems and Commentary* (Cambridge, MA: Harvard University Press, 2010), 187.

8. Cynthia Griffin Wolff, *Emily Dickinson* (New York: Alfred A. Knopf, 1986), 397.

9. Martha Dickinson Bianchi, *Emily Dickinson: Face to Face* (Boston: Houghton Mifflin, 1932), 66.

10. Ibid., 46.

11. Vendler, *Dickinson: Selected Poems and Commentary*, 337.

THREE: ASCETICISM

1. Richard Wilbur, "Sumptuous Destitution," in *Emily Dickinson: A Collection of Critical Essays*, ed. Richard Sewall (Englewood Cliffs, NJ: Prentice Hall, 1963), 135.

2. Sally Cunneen, preface to *The Imitation of Christ* by Thomas à Kempis, ed. and trans. Joseph N. Tylenda, SJ (New York: Random House, 1998), xvii.

3. Thomas à Kempis, *The Imitation of Christ*, 4.

4. Antoine de Saint-Exupéry, *The Little Prince*, trans. Katherine Woods (San Diego: Harcourt Brace, 1943), 87.

5. Thomas à Kempis, *The Imitation of Christ*, 5.

6. Ibid., 26.

7. Ibid., 63–67.

8. Cunneen, preface, ibid., xvii–xix.

9. Nathaniel Hawthorne, *The Marble Faun* (Boston: Houghton, Mifflin, 1883), 71.

10. Cynthia Griffin Wolff, *Emily Dickinson* (New York: Alfred A. Knopf, 1986), 395.

FOUR: PLACE

1. Michael Kelly, Marta L. Werner, Carolyn Vega, Susan Howe, and Richard Wilbur, *The Networked Recluse: The Connected World of Emily Dickinson* (Amherst, MA: Amherst College Press, 2017).

2. Wallace Stevens, *Esthétique du Mal*, in *The Collected Poems* (New York: Alfred A. Knopf, 1954), 286.

3. Cynthia Griffin Wolff, *Emily Dickinson* (New York: Alfred A. Knopf, 1986), 143.

4. Pope Francis, *Laudato Si': On Care for Our Common Home* (Huntington, IN: OSV Press, 2015), 9.

5. Gilbert of Hoyland, *Sermons on the Song of Songs*, trans. Lawrence C. Braceland (Collegeville, MN: Cistercian Publications, 1978), 122–23.

6. Benedict XVI, *Acta Apostolicae Sedis* 97.711, April 24, 2005.

7. Pope Francis, *Laudato Si'*, 84–85.

8. Ibid., 234.

9. Wolff, *Emily Dickinson*, 531.

10. Ibid., 505.

FIVE: THE DESIRE FOR LOVE

1. Benedict XVI, *Deus Caritas Est* (Boston: Pauline Books, 2006), 7.

2. Ibid., 10.

3. Iain Matthew, *The Impact of God: Soundings from St. John of the Cross* (London: Hadder & Stoughton, 1995), 38.

4. Ibid., 65.

5. Helen Vendler, *Dickinson: Selected Poems and Commentary* (Cambridge, MA: Harvard University Press, 2010), 264–65.

6. Richard Wilbur, in *Emily Dickinson: A Collection of Critical Essays*, ed. Richard Sewall (Englewood Cliffs, NJ: Prentice Hall, 1963), 134.

SIX: THE FEAR OF DEATH

1. Pope Francis, *Laudato Si'* (Huntington, IN: OSV Press, 2015), 243.

2. Cynthia Griffin Wolff, *Emily Dickinson* (New York: Alfred A. Knopf, 1986), 264.

3. Karl Rahner, "Relationship between Nature and Grace: The Supernatural Existential," in *A Rahner Reader*, ed. Gerald McCool (New York: Crossroad, 1975), 187.

CONCLUSION

1. Teresa of Ávila, *Life*, in *The Complete Works of Saint Teresa of Jesus*, trans. E. Allison Peers (New York: Sheed & Ward, 1944), 1:58.

2. Julia Kristeva, *Teresa, My Love: An Imagined Life of the Saint of Avila*, trans. Lorna Scott Fox (New York: Columbia, 2008), 64.

3. Ibid., 189.

4. Augustine, *The Confessions*, trans. John K. Ryan (New York: Doubleday Image, 1960), 254.

5. Teresa of Ávila, *Interior Castle*, trans. and ed. E. Allison Peers (New York: Doubleday Image, 1988), 104–5.

6. George Eliot, *Middlemarch* (New York: Modern Library, 1994), 1.

7. Kristeva, *Teresa, My Love*, 193.

8. Cynthia Griffin Wolff, *Emily Dickinson* (New York: Alfred A. Knopf, 1986), 143.

9. Kristeva, *Teresa, My Love*, 425.

10. Martha Dickinson Bianchi, *Emily Dickinson: Face to Face* (Boston: Houghton Mifflin, 1932), 63–64.

11. Ibid., 91.

12. Teresa of Ávila, *Life*, 150.

13. Richard B. Sewall, *The Life of Emily Dickinson* (New York: Farrar, Straus & Giroux, 1974), 2:700.

14. Jasper Hopkins, *Nicholas of Cusa's Dialectical Mysticism* (Minneapolis: Arthur J. Banning, 1988), 129–30.

15. Benedict XVI with Peter Seewald, *Last Testament: In His Own Words* (London: Bloomsbury, 2016), 238.

16. Quoted in Peter John Cameron, *Benedictus: Day by Day with Pope Benedict XVI* (Yonkers, NY: Magnificat, 2006), 271.

17. Wallace Stevens, "Of Mere Being," in *Opus Posthumous*, ed. Milton J. Bates (New York: Alfred A. Knopf, 1989), 141. Copyright © 1957 by Elsie Stevens and Holly Stevens. Used by permission of Alfred A. Knopf, an imprint of the Knopf Doubleday Publishing Group, a division of Penguin Random House LLC. All rights reserved. United Kingdom and Commonwealth (excluding Canada) rights in process.

18. Catherine of Siena, *The Dialogue*, trans. Suzanne Noffke, OP (New York: Paulist Press, 1980), 363.